British Costumes

PYNE'S

British Costumes

An illustrated survey of early eighteenth-century dress in the British Isles, written and designed by

WILLIAM H. PYNE

Wordsworth Editions

*This edition published 1989 by Wordsworth Editions Ltd,
8b East Street, Ware, Hertfordshire.*

ISBN 1-85326-926-3

Printed and bound in Spain by Gráficas Estella SA.

PUBLISHER'S PREFACE.

As civilization and mental improvement advance in any country, a laudable curiosity is awakened to enquire into, and become acquainted with, the appearance, manners, and opinions of other nations.

To satisfy this curiosity,—and to store the mind with the useful and pleasing information that is derived from a comparison of the sentiments, customs, and even prejudices of the inhabitants of countries living under different forms of government; influenced by dissimilar modes of education; and conducting their public and domestic concerns upon principles of various, and often contradictory, tendency;—those who have not the means and opportunity of travelling themselves, must be content to receive the assistance of others; who visit the inhabitants of various countries, and consign, through the medium of the pencil and the pen, the results of their observations, to the instruction and amusement of those who pass not the barrier of their native land.

The legislator, the statesman, and the philosopher look to the traveller whose pages exhibit the political, statistical, and literary characteristics of the countries passed through; and who examine the causes and develope the effects that conduce to the wealth, prosperity, and independence of states;—but a very numerous class of enquirers confine not their attention to these difficult and weighty investigations;—they wish to be informed respecting the individual manner, the external appearance, and the general character of different countries; and for these amusing and instructive purposes the works called COSTUMES OF VARIOUS NATIONS are admirably adapted.

By presenting to the eye a series of judiciously selected and well executed pictorial representations, forming striking portraits of single subjects, accurately finished in the colours of the original, and aided by short descriptive essays, they give more pleasing and definite ideas of the external character, style of dress, and peculiarity of occupation, than can be acquired by any other method, except actual personal observation.

The Publisher of this Work having at great labour and expence produced a series of Costumes, illustrative of the Manners, Habits, and Decorations of several highly interesting Foreign Countries, with which British travellers and British readers have been, till of late years, very little conversant, thought that the utility and interest of the whole might be considerably augmented by contrasting them with similar representations taken from his own country:—with this view, therefore, the following COSTUMES OF ENGLAND have been executed. In a country presenting such an infinite variety of interesting subjects, the only difficulty has been to compress the Volume within moderate bounds. In making this selection, it has been attempted to include all classes of society; and delineations are therefore given from the most elevated ranks of public functionaries, to the lowest gradation of mechanic and laborious avocation; and it is hoped the execution of this Work will be found not undeserving of the same high character, with which public approbation hath already stamped the FOREIGN COSTUMES; and which may be considered still more interesting and complete by the addition of those of GREAT BRITAIN.

As it is possible this Volume may fall into the hands of those who are unacquainted with the publications on Foreign Costume above alluded to, they are therefore here enumerated:

TABLE OF CONTENTS.

PLATE I.

POTTERY.

THE useful and elegant art of pottery is of great antiquity: convenience alone, it is likely, dictated the operations of those who first formed vessels of clay; but as facility of execution disposes the mind to improvement, it is not improbable that ornamental works of this material were produced among the early efforts of human ingenuity. The Egyptians excelled in this art: and there are various beautiful allusions to the potter, interspersed in the Sacred Writings.

The many antique vases, lamps, ornaments, and utensils of sacrifice, &c. discovered during the last century in the subterraneous researches made in Italy and Greece, prove what exquisite perfection this art had attained near three thousand years ago. The Chinese trace their knowledge of pottery to very high antiquity. The manufacture of porcelaine was practised by them as early as the fifth century: it was for ages made entirely colourless, when they discovered that a deep blue, a species of lapis lazuli, would unite withit. This they employed for many years in ornamenting their ware, till perseverance in experiment at length enabled them to enamel their works with all the teints of the rainbow. The process for making this china, they preserved with impenetrable secresy for several centuries; its fame, however, spreading, and the demand for it increasing in the different parts of the world, induced the ingenious of various countries to attempt the discovery, and many men highly eminent for science exerted themselves in the pursuit. The clue to this secret was, no doubt, given by the Jesuit missionaries, sent to China by the Duke of Tuscany: but the Saxons claim the honour of making the discovery; the Dresden ware having been the first of European manufacture, which soon attained such perfection as to possess some qualities superior to the true china, and produce larger prices. Since this, manufactories have been established for making porcelaine in most European countries, and with various success. The Dresden china has long been celebrated; the French is famous for its admirable whiteness; Italy has produced excellent copies of the antique figures by this process; Delft, in Holland, established a ware, which experienced an extensive circulation; and England, in addition to her various manufactures of china ware, which are much admired, has had the honour of restoring to the world the process of making the antique pottery in imitation of the Etruscan and Greek. We owe the

Published January 1.1805 by William Miller Albemarle Street.

revival of this invaluable branch of that art to the ingenuity of Mr. Josiah Wedgewood, who, with the assistance of Mr. Bentley, analized every fragment of the antique he could procure, with unceasing perseverance, till the discovery was complete. Since which time, the modern Etruria has sent out an immense number of urns, vases, figures, vessels, and ornaments, composed with great spirit and beauty, and executed with surprising delicacy. He engaged artists of high repute to make copies of the finest specimens of the antique, and also to model original classic works, which were manufactured of various texture. Hence our houses are now decorated with ornaments, the simplicity and grace of which have contributed in a high degree to the improvement of the public taste.

Formerly a great passion existed, in this country, for collecting vases, jars, cups, and other ornaments of porcelaine, which were purchased at immense prices; some of the jars were several feet high. It was customary to have them in the apartments of the great; and ladies placed Chinese vases in their dressing-rooms, filled with odoriferous herbs and flowers. There were collectors of Delft ware also: a pair of jars of this ware, and of no great magnitude, has produced three hundred guineas at a sale. This taste for the grotesque forms of the Chinese, happily gave place to the beauty and justness of proportion so obvious in the antique, and the China ornament is now principally confined to the museum of the virtuoso.

The subject of this plate is employed in making the red pottery, and was selected, in preference to any other, from the picturesque simplicity of the wheel, &c.

Published January 1, 1805, by William Miller, Albemarle Street.

PLATE II.

TANNING.

THE manufacture of leather is a branch of business, by which the English have acquired reputation in foreign markets. Their tanned leather is held in particular esteem, being allowed to possess a greater degree of durability, and to resist water better than that of any other country.

The process for tanning leather is tedious though simple, as it takes some months to complete. Many attempts have been made here, and on the Continent of Europe, particularly in France, to discover a method of performing that operation in a shorter period; but notwithstanding several persons, eminent for their chemical knowledge, assisted in the pursuit, and devoted much time to experiments, yet no means have been ascertained comparable with the simple and ancient method. The essential part of the process is, after the hair is taken from the hides, and they have undergone a certain preparation, to place them in pits, or oozes, filled with a solution of oak-bark. It is likely that the English tanned leather owes its superiority, in a great measure, to the excellent quality of the bark, which is the production of our own soil. The hides of horses, bulls, cows, and calves, are tanned by this method. The skins of deer, sheep, and lambs, are dressed with oil, and comprise what is called oil leather. White leather is dressed by another process, and comprises dog, sheep, goat, kid, and lamb skins. Vast quantities of skins are annually imported into this country, and after being manufactured in various ways, with much care and skill, are exported to different parts of the globe. An extensive commerce is carried on with America in the skin and fur trade. February 9, 1804, were sold, at the New York Coffee-house, 250,595 deer-skins; and on the 7th and 8th of March following, 154,030 racoon, 33,420 black bears, 408 brown and gray bears, 645 Russian bears, 47,670 sable, 20,940 otter, 8,080 fisher, 15,170 lynx cats, 26,640 mink, 5,960 wolf, 14,360 fox, 1,330 wolverine, 87,850 musquaoh, 22,100 rabbits.

This trade has been practised for many centuries, and several laws that existed relating to it, were revised in the reign of James the First. Of their privileges, it is said, " no person shall be a tanner who hath not served seven years, except the wife of such a tanner, or hath used the trade four years, or the son or daughter of a tanner, or such person who shall marry such wife or daughter, to whom he shall leave a tan-house and fats ; on pain of forfeiting all such leather tanned, or of which he shall receive any profit or the value thereof." To deter them from a practice then in use, similar to what has been attempted in foreign countries, " no person shall set fats in tan-hills or other places, where the oozes or leather may take unkind heats, or shall put any leather into any hot or warm oozes, on pain of ten pounds, and the pillory on three market-days, in the next market-town."

The figure represented in this Plate is termed a feltmonger, which is a branch of tanning.

The figures in the back-ground are employed in frizing, or removing the hair from the skins, which is performed by laying them upon a beam, and scraping them with an arched iron instrument. Few places produce appearances more picturesque than a tanner's, or feltmonger's yard. The ooze-pits, for the hides, the pumps, troughs, and rude implements, and above all, the dress and various employments of the workmen, afford many excellent subjects for the pencil.

Published by William Miller, Albemarle Street, Jan.y 1, 1805.

PLATE III.

YEOMEN OF THE KING'S BODY-GUARD.

THIS guard owes its establishment to the suspicions of Henry VII., who, dreading some attempt upon his person, provided a band of fifty archers, clothing them in an uniform of scarlet broad-cloth, embroidered with lace: they were chosen from among a class immediately below the gentry, and being raised expressly to attend upon his person, were denominated Yeomen of the King's Body-Guard. Henry possessed too much discernment to suppose this new corps could be raised without exciting his subjects' apprehensions: indeed, the nation ever regarded them with jealous watchfulness, and they were not augmented during his reign. Another corps of yeomanry existed as early as the reign of Edward III., which has been frequently mistaken for this guard; but they attended the king only at the time of insurrection, or on foreign service, were termed Yeomen of the Crown, and disbanded in the reign of Charles. It is probable, the Yeoman-Guard were with Henry VII. at the siege of Boulogne; it is certain they were with Henry VIII. at the celebrated battle of Spurs, and at the siege of Tournay; for, upon their return from that campaign, Henry bestowed pensions upon them for their good conduct, with an exemption from attendance on his person, or at court, but on particular occasions. Cardinal Wolsey sometimes retained a part of this corps to add to the splendour of his pageantries, though he had a body-guard of his own; but he did not imitate his sovereign's munificence towards them, for during the time of a mortality in London, Henry removed, with a small retinue, to Eltham, where he kept his Christmas (termed the still-Christmas). The Cardinal, taking advantage of this circumstance, set about curtailing the King's household, and dismissed amongst the rest eight-four of this guard, reducing them to great distress. Some time after, the Yeomen-Guard had an opportunity of witnessing this proud prelate's reverse of fortune, for twenty-four of them were dispatched, under Sir William Kingston, to bring him to London, to answer charges preferred against him for high-treason; but he died upon the road. This king sometimes mixed in the amusements of his subjects, under the disguise of the Yeoman's dress, and thereby became acquainted with their sentiments regarding himself. During this reign, the Yeoman's Guard was augmented and reduced, according to state necessity, but never mustered fewer than two hundred. Soon after the accession of Mary to the throne, this corps received an augmentation, making the number four hundred and seven, exclusive of thirty Yeomen of the Crown. At the same time the dress received the addition of rich embroidery. Her personal safety, still endangered by the remnant of Northumberland's faction, seems to have caused so great an addition to be made to the Yeoman's Guard. No material alteration appears to have taken place with them till the reign of Charles I., and during the Commonwealth they were disbanded; but at the Restoration they were re-embodied, and settled at one hundred, with officers, &c., in nearly the same order as they now remain. Six of this corps are termed Yeomen-hangers, and two Yeomen-bedgoers, whose departments are to have charge of his Majesty's camp equipage when he takes the field. They pitched a tent of cloth of gold for the Emperor Maximilian, who acted as a volunteer under Henry VIII., at the camp near Tournay. Baker says, "As no king was ever served by such a soldier, so no soldier ever lodged in such a tent." The last time this corps left England, was when George II. went to command the army at Hanover. One half the corps were formerly mounted on horses, and were armed with the harquebus; the foot carried the partizan. After the demise of King William, the harquebus was laid aside. They wore red stockings so late as the reign of George II.

This corps has a captain, lieutenant, ensign, clerks of the cheque, four exons, eight yeomen-ushers, six yeomen-hangers, and two yeomen-bedgoers: they keep a guard of thirty, day and night, at the Palace of St. James's; have two rooms allotted to them, ornamented with various arms, called the King's and the Queen's Guard Chambers; and a table is furnished daily, for all those upon duty, from the kitchen of his Majesty.

A guard of forty yeomen-warders is maintained at the Tower of London, which was established by Henry VIII. during his residence there, at the beginning of his reign: their services, however, are limited to that fortress. They were reduced to twenty-four in the reign of Charles II.; but King William restored them to their original number. Their dress is the same as the King's Guard at St. James's, excepting the carbine belt, which they are not allowed to wear.

Published by William Miller, Albemarle Street, Jany. 1805.

PLATE IV.

A FIREMAN.

THE earliest establishment in this country of insurance from loss by fire, of which we have any certain account, was projected in 1560, by a set of merchants from Lombardy; but the scheme was confined to ships of commerce, and their cargoes. The same persons also established the system of lending money upon pledges, as pawn-brokers. It is said the invention is of Roman origin, a species of insurance having been created in the reign of Claudius. The Jews in this country are reputed to have used a custom for mutual indemnification from accidents by fire, six hundred years since. The Hand-in-Hand office was the first created for insuring houses, opened in 1696, and enrolled in Chancery in 1698. The Sun fire-office opened in 1710, but on a more extensive plan, including houses, furniture, goods, &c. The Union-office appeared in 1714, for insurance of goods only; the London, and Royal-Exchange offices opened in the same year, 1716, for houses, goods, &c.; and the Westminster in 1717. Thus, in a few years from the foundation of the Hand-in-Hand, was established a system of insurance, on so extensive a plan as to enable persons to secure the amount of their property from the ravages of fire, at the low rate of a few shillings for a hundred pounds. It remained, however, for the Phœnix company to complete this grand scheme; for, prior to their plan, opened in 1782, certain manufactories, buildings, and commodities, subject to great risk from fire, were not admitted to the benefit of insurance in any office. This firm opened policies which included every species of property, and regulated the premium in proportion to the risk, classing the articles under the terms of hazardous, doubly hazardous, &c. thereby rendering security to such persons as were most exposed to suffer from that destructive element. Three other offices have arisen since the Phœnix; the Imperial, Globe, and British. The emblem of the Hand-in-Hand, adopted by the first company, is highly characteristic of so laudable an institution, and the result has eminently proved the estimable consequences arising from an union of persons associating for mutual benefit.

The page of history has recorded many instances of the dreadful ravages made by fire, upon the lives and property of the inhabitants of this country, London alone having been nearly destroyed five times. The first upon record happened in the reign of Ethelred II.,

982; also in the reigns of William Rufus, 1087; the Empress Maude, 1132; Stephen, 1136: and Charles II., 1666. This last memorable conflagration pointed out the necessity of forming some plan for alleviating the misfortunes of future sufferers. It is not easy for the mind to conceive the complicated distress which followed this calamity. One prodigious difficulty arose in arranging the claims of landlords and tenants, the sites of many premises being totally obliterated; and it is likely few deeds or papers escaped the flames during the general consternation. The litigations referring to these claims might have been endless, but for the interference of the legislature, who appointed twenty-two judges, who sat constantly to determine differences, without expense to the parties; and by their great wisdom and equity, this weighty business was arranged to the entire satisfaction of all claimants. The City, in gratitude for these services, placed their portraits, painted at full length, in Guildhall.

The subject of this Plate is in the dress of the Sun fire-office; the pick-axe and fire-cap denote the active duties of his occupation: the cap is of horse-hide, strengthened with cross-bars of metal; the inside is of leather, quilted and stuffed with wool, to protect the head from falling bricks, or spars, which firemen are frequently exposed to during the violence of a fire. Great emulation is excited amongst them by the shouting of the populace; and the intrepid exertions of many of these useful men, in endeavouring to check the progress of the flames, have unfortunately in too many instances proved fatal to themselves.

Several ingenious inventions have been suggested, and experiments made for extinguishing fire in buildings, &c., but with little success. None has appeared to answer the purpose equally with the fire-engine. The best of these machines will throw water over lofty buildings, and with such velocity as to force, through a branch or pipe three-fourths of an inch diameter, a tun of water in a minute. They have been in use about one hundred and fifty years; but of late have received considerable improvement. A representation of one of these machines is introduced in the back-ground to this subject.

PLATE V.

WOMAN SELLING SALOP.

THE different ranks of society in every country have some customs peculiar to themselves; but the distance existing between the higher and lower classes in a civilized state is so remote, in many instances, as to render them almost ignorant of each other's habits of life.

At a very early hour of the morning may be seen, in various parts of the streets of London, the humble venders of salop, with their bright scowered kettles, steaming with that wholesome beverage, surrounded by groups of men and women, whose avocations expose them to the vicissitudes of the weather the whole year round. These people attend their stalls, as early as three or four o'clock in the morning, and deal out gingerbread and warm salop to their shivering customers, in many a wintry storm.

He who wishes to study the manners, and note the modes of life of the inhabitants of this great metropolis, must extend his observations beyond the court, the bar, the theatre, or the Exchange. A mutual dependence binds the society together; and the honest exertions of the meanest member is of consequence to the whole. Many a scene replete with interest has commenced, and a very industrious and useful class of the community have been busily employed hours before the affluent leave their beds. Such is the contrast; that the fruitress may be going to Covent Garden market to purchase vegetables and fruit, whilst the fishmonger is driving his caravan to Billingsgate for fish; the milk people, with their clanging pails, are on their way to the cow-farm; and the infant chimney-sweeper is raising his shrill voice to gain admittance, where he is to ply his ignominious drudgery, at the same moment when the nobleman is still engaged at the gaming-table, and the lady of fashion is stepping into her sedan, to be carried home to her couch.

Published by William Miller, Albemarle Street, Jan.y 1. 1805.

No. 6.

PLATE VI.

HERALD.

THE College of Heralds has existed from the reign of Richard the Third to the present time. Charles the Sixth of France incorporated the officers at arms of that country in the year 1406; and it is supposed Richard was influenced by his example, as shortly after his assumption to the throne, this establishment commenced. The services of these officers at arms were particularly necessary to a prince of his turbulent disposition; for, during this short reign, they are frequently mentioned in parlies with his opponents; it is likely many of them were attached to his cause, for after the battle of Bosworth Field, we find among the list of persons attainted for assisting therein, the name Richard Watkins, Herald at Arms. Windsor Herald, however, was retained by the Duke of Richmond, and dispatched to the Lord Mayor of York, to notify the death of the tyrant Richard, and defeat of his army, and of the elevation of the Duke of Richmond, his conqueror, to the throne, by the title of Henry the Seventh, proclaiming the same by right of his office. These tidings were unwelcome to the city of York; but making a merit of necessity, they received the news with a tolerable grace. The Heralds derive their names from the Anglo-Saxons; their titles, anciently, were Dukes at Arms. The title of Garter, King at Arms, was created by Henry the Fifth, in whose time the magnificence of the state was much attended to: Chivalry was carried to a romantic height by this prince, as it had been in the reign of Edward the Third.

The titles of the Kings at Arms, in the different reigns, have been Surroy or Southroy, Norroy or Northroy, Clarenceux, Ireland, Aquitaine, Vollant or Vaillant, March, Lancaster, Falcon, Guienne, Agincourt, and others: of Heralds at Arms, Windsor, Carlisle, Chester, Leicester, York, Falcon, Ulster, Lancaster, Hereford, Richmond, Norfolk, Arundel, Suffolk, Nottingham, Brunswick, Blanc Courser, &c. Pursuivants, Rouge Dragon, Portcullis, Rouge Croix, Blue Mantle, Comfort, Rose Blanch, Calais, Berwick, Blanch Sanglier, Athlone, Hampnes, Risebank, Rouge Rôse, Blanch Lion, Newhaven, Portsmouth, &c. The persons of the Heralds were held sacred; they were employed in negociations of the greatest importance; they were the messengers of peace and war, making public proclamation of the same; they were deputed to carry challenges to princes and generals at the head of the enemies' army; summoned besieged places to surrender; and covered from assault persons placed under their protection, bearing messages from the enemy to the field of battle or the camp; they published victories, and made returns of the slain, and were frequently dispatched to the court with the tidings of victory.

At coronations, marriages, baptisms, and funerals of the royal family, at the interviews of sovereign princes, and at the magnificent royal banquets of former times, the kings at arms and heralds made a conspicuous figure; possessed of many privileges, their influence was great, and their services have been highly useful to the state. Men esteemed for talents and virtue have worn the tabard: Camden and Dugdale were both of this respectable corps.

At tilts and tournaments, when the king or any of the royal family were present, the heralds attended, who read the challenge. They were with the monarch, also, at the court, the senate, and the field. All grants of arms, whether for the nobility, or gentry, were regulated by them.

Brugge Garter, (in the reign of Henry the Fifth) had the honour to entertain the Emperor Sigismund, at his seat at Kentish Town. In the reign of Henry the Seventh, Lyon, King at Arms, was sent from the Scottish camp with a challenge from James the Fourth to the Duke of Norfolk, offering to fight him in a single combat, to prevent the effusion of Christian blood. Prior to the celebrated battle of Flodden Field, in the reign of Henry the Eighth, the Earl of Surry sent a challenge to the same King, who had taken a position for his camp by the side of a hill, on a spot naturally strong, and rendered more so by art and artillery: the English General could not make the attack but with manifest disadvantage; but knowing that the Scottish monarch possessed most romantic notions of courage, he sent Rouge Croix, Pursuivant, with a trumpet, bearing a most taunting and provoking challenge, inviting him to come and join in battle; which James accepted, contrary to the advice of his officers, saying, had he received such a message in his own castle of Edinburgh, he would have left it to have fought the English army. The army of the brave but unfortunate monarch was defeated, and himself was slain. The same Pursuivant is mentioned in a letter written by the Queen Regent to Henry, who was then besieging Tournay, to notify the defeat of the Scottish army. "My husband, for hasteness of Rouge Crosse, I could not send your Grace the piece of King of Scots coat; I thought to send himself to you, but our Englishmen would not suffer it."

The dress of the Heralds is similar to that worn in the time of King Richard, as appears by the Warwick roll, (a curious manuscript in the Heralds College,) wherein is represented the illustrious chiefs of that family, and among them the portrait, at full length, of Richard, in the tabard, embroidered with the arms of England and France.

Published Jany. 1st. 1805, by William Miller, Albemarle Street. No. 6.

PLATE VII.

CHELSEA PENSIONER.

A GERMAN potentate, whose magnanimity was celebrated by certain poets and historians of his time, caused an order to be issued in his camp, forbidding the performance of amputation upon the limbs of his brave soldiers who were left wounded upon the field of battle, wishing to avoid burthening the state with useless members. Yet attempting to cloak this cruel act of state parsimony by an affectation of sympathizing in their sufferings! Happily here the soldier who has been deprived of his limbs in battle, or the aged veteran enfeebled by long service, is not considered as a burthen to the state; he that has patiently endured the scorching heat of the East, or the piercing cold of the North; who has bravely faced danger in all the horror of war, returns not to an ungrateful country, exposed to poverty and neglect: an asylum is provided for the repose of his aching limbs, in the noble Military Hospital at Chelsea, where many a gray-headed veteran

> " Sinks to the grave with unperceived decay,
> " Whilst resignation gently slopes the way."

The dress worn by those who are clothed by public bounty, far from appearing a mark of reproach, becomes the passport to every good man's esteem. Who can have passed the aged soldier in the uniform of a Chelsea pensioner, without having felt a sentiment of respect glowing in his bosom, as a pleasing tribute due to the defender of his country?

In this Hospital are accommodations for several hundred aged and disabled soldiers, who are provided with board, clothing, and all the necessaries of life. Their dress is composed of a red coat, lined with blue, great coat, waistcoat, breeches and stockings of blue also. The building is admirably designed for the purposes of an Hospital, having several wards, airy, and of an amazing size, allowing every man his separate cabin; the aged and infirm have their ward upon the ground floor, being spared the fatigue of ascending the stairs; indeed every accommodation consistent with their humble rank is afforded them. Many instances of longevity may be gathered from the annals of this College. The cleanliness, sobriety, and temperate habits of the establishment, the healthiness of the site, and the benevolent attention of the medical department, contribute much to lengthen their days; indeed as much solicitude is shown for the recovery of any of its humble inhabitants when in the infirmary, as could be felt did the physician receive his regular fees.

This establishment makes a certain provision, also, for several thousand disabled soldiers and superannuated veterans, as out-pensioners, by allowing each seven pounds twelve shillings and sixpence a year: It is greatly to be lamented that a number of these brave men are not provided with accommodations somewhat similar to those afforded in the Hospital; as many of them are very improvident; and that which was so humanely intended to add to their comfort, is too frequently dissipated in drunkenness and debauchery; or seduced from them by needy relations, or designing companions. This, it is humbly suggested, might be accomplished without erecting so magnificent a pile for their reception, and the places of those who died in Chelsea College might be filled up from the list of the most orderly and deserving of the new establishment. The additional expenses accruing from such a provision, it is presumed, would be cheerfully contributed by a people grateful for their past services. It is pleasing to reflect on the pension which has been bestowed upon the brave soldiers who lost their sight in the memorable campaign in Egypt: Yet should it appear that they are occasionally fleeced of their pittance, how wretched, how hopeless must their state become.

The expenses of this grand national establishment are supported by a poundage deducted out of the pay of the army, with one day's pay annually from each officer and common soldier; and when there is any deficiency, it is supplied by a sum raised by parliament. This Hospital is governed by the following persons: the President of the Council, the First Commissioner of the Treasury, the principal Secretary of State, the Paymaster General of the Forces, the Secretary at War, the Comptrollers of the Army, and by the Governor and Lieutenant Governor of the Hospital. The expense of erecting this College, &c. amounted to one hundred and fifty thousand pounds, and the site occupied is forty acres.

Published by William Miller, Albemarle Street, Jan.y 1. 1805.

No. 8.

PLATE VIII.

WARDMOTE INQUEST.

AMONG the many wholesome laws made by our countrymen of old, for the suppression of fraud, stand conspicuous those which were formed for regulating the standard of weights and measures; but though the utmost vigilance was exerted by the officers appointed to superintend this department of the police, yet it appears the propensity to cheating was so great among traders, that severe penalties were enacted, and punishments multiplied to oblige them to be honest. The goldsmith's company were permitted the privilege of assaying precious metals when wrought into ornaments, utensils, trinkets, &c.; the leathersellers that of inspecting the quality of hides; the aleconners the trying of wines and other liquors; and various trades and callings had their inspectors; all these officers being governed by a code of regulations, highly creditable to the wisdom of the legislators and magistrates of these early times.

Formerly most of the necessary articles of consumption were vended in public markets; the hurry and confusion attendant upon such numerous assemblies must have exposed people to great impositions; to prevent which, public weighing-beams were erected in different parts of the metropolis, which were attended by officers called weigh-masters, at whose beam all commodities sold might be reweighed, by which frauds were not only discovered, but the commission of many, also, prevented. We find as early as Edward the Second, that a petition was preferred to that monarch, for leave to erect a weighing-beam in the churchyard of St. Mary, Woolchurch, (near Stock's Market) for the purpose of taking tronage, or tonnage upon wool, and for weighing all other commodities by the city weigh-master, who was to see justice done between buyer and seller. Before the salutary laws of Charles the Second were enacted for regulating the markets, the standard for each diocese was held by the bishop, who appointed a priest to preside over the market of his town, empowering him to see that justice was done to each party, to assay the weights and measures, and to fine those who trespassed against the law; hence arose the custom and title of clerk of the market.

Weights and measures have been invented near three thousand years, the standard for which is of great antiquity; the Jews placed theirs in the sanctuary, under the care of the priests; the Romans had the same custom; and the original standard of our weights and measures is deposited in the Exchequer.

When the laws of assize were settled in the reign of William the Conqueror, the pound was fixed at twelve ounces (as used by the Saxons); and in the reign of King John, an act was made to prohibit the use of any other weight throughout the realm. In Henry the Seventh's reign, the pound troy, being three quarters of an ounce more than the Saxon, was established: but the great change commenced in the reign of his son; for what had long been a custom in many parts, was confirmed by a statute of Henry the Eighth; namely, that butchers and others should be obliged to use a pound of sixteen ounces, (termed the avoirdupois,) since which time it has been in general use for weighing all those commodities comprised under the title of garbel, as all kinds of grocery wares, drugs, butter, cheese, flesh, wax, pitch, tar, tallow, wool, hemp, flax, iron, steel, lead, and all other commodities from which issueth a refuse or waste; and twelve pounds over are allowed to every hundred. Bread is also weighed by this custom, by an act of George the Second, but prior to that reign, it was regulated by the pound troy; by which weight now are sold silk, gold, silver, pearl, and precious stones.

"Troy weight is by law, avoirdupois by custom, yet confirmed by statute." By the twelfth of Henry the Seventh, "every bushel shall contain eight gallons of wheat, and every gallon eight pounds troy, and every pound twelve ounces, on the penalty of £20 upon every city, borough, town, or place having the keeping of common measures, that shall keep any other bushel or gallon." The legal Winchester bushel, according to the standard in the Exchequer, shall be round, with a plain bottom eighteen inches and a half wide throughout, and eight inches deep.

Also, "that the mayors and other head officers in market towns shall, twice a year or oftener, cause all weights and measures within the same to be brought before them, and examined; and such as they find defective, to be broken and burnt; and the offender shall forfeit to the mayor or other officer, for the first time, six shillings and eight pence: for the second time, thirteen and fourpence; and the third time, twenty shillings, and be set on the pillory." The penalties relating to this heinous offence have been mitigated during the present reign, though the immorality of the act calls for a severe punishment.

The figure in this Plate represents one of the Wardmote Inquest in the dress of his office; each ward has its inquest, the members of which are chosen from among the most respectable inhabitants, and the establishment is peculiar to the city of London. We read of their existence as early as 1383, the seventh of Richard the Second, who punished all night-walkers and disorderly persons, by confining them in a prison called the tun. The power of this inquest is extensive, as the regulating several branches of the police falls to their department, one material part of which is the assaying of weights and measures.

PLATE IX.

WELSH PEASANTS WASHING.

THE custom of beating the linen with a wooden spatula, as represented in this Plate, is not confined to the Welsh; as the same method is used in many parts of France. The washers assemble by the side of a clear and rapid stream; and after rinsing their linen, or woollen, select a smooth flat stone, upon which it is placed, and beaten till it becomes clean; it is afterwards spread upon the rocks or grass, and left to dry.

The Scottish peasants have a method of washing their linen by a very different process, called bucking; after having soaked it, an active lass, with her clothes curiously tucked between her knees, gets into the tub, and treads the wash with her naked feet; two women frequently are seen treading in the same tub, and by placing their hands upon each other's shoulders, perform this operation with much agility and great ease.

There are few prettier or more interesting embellishments for landscape scenery to be met with than those which occur by the side of the Welsh mountain streams; the peasants form the most picturesque assemblage of all that can charm in that delightful study.

The dresses worn by the Welch peasantry are very different from the English, being principally of woollen, striped, checked, &c.; the women are accustomed to wrap their heads in handkerchiefs, over which they wear men's hats; the general character of the whole is much in the style of the Flemish peasants.

These mountaineers are very strong; great numbers of them, particularly the females, walk to London in the summer season, when they are employed by the gardeners in its vicinity, to carry baskets of strawberries to Covent Garden market: it is a most laborious service, but their strength and spirits enable them to accomplish it; and after working some time at weeding, &c. they return to Wales, happy with the earnings acquired by their honesty and labour.

THE BEST
BOOTH
in the

PLATE X.

A COUNTRY FAIR.

THE itinerant who is represented upon the little stage, is the inventor of the ingenious method of ringing the changes alone upon a set of hand bells, which were cast by himself, and are extremely musical in their tones: there is much mechanical skill displayed in their structure, as the clappers are prevented by springs, from bearing upon their sides to preserve the vibration, and they strike transversely: great ingenuity is exhibited also in the use of them; and when it is considered how few there are endowed with the ability to add any thing original to the public stock of innocent amusement, it is likely this humble mechanic might have distinguished himself, had his talents been directed to a higher employment.

Hand bells, of late years, have been introduced in dramatic performances with very pretty effect; the custom originated with the subject of the Plate: When Garrick's Jubilee, in honour of our immortal bard, appeared upon Drury-lane stage, its great success excited the envy of the managers of the other house, till at length they were induced to burlesque it, under the title of Harlequin's Jubilee; wherein appeared this player upon the hand bells; he was borne upon the shoulders of eight men, in a grand triumphal car, and wore a superb dress. As a specimen of the success attendant upon folly, it is asserted, that this piece was represented forty nights in succession, to crowded houses!

A few years ago, an ideot made a structure of wood about twenty feet high, in rude imitation of a church; in which he had the ingenuity to hang a set of small bells, with lines to pull them; and he was directed by his ear, to imitate the changes rung upon the bells in the neighbouring steeple;* which he performed with correctness, both as to time and variety; in this place he would pass most of his time, in a state of happiness that excited much sympathy. He appeared to be about twenty-five years of age, was very harmless, and had never exhibited symptoms of reason in any other instance from his childhood.

Bell ringing was a custom peculiar to the English in the middle ages. Hand bells, according to Mr. Strutt, first appeared in the religious processions, and were afterwards used by the secular musi-

* Christ Church, Surry.

cians, and practised for the sake of pastime. The notions of music as a science must have been very low about the time of Richard the Second: King David, in his diadem and royal robes, was represented playing upon five small bells, with a little hammer in each hand, the bells are suspended to an ornamental stand; this was painted upon a curious manuscript, and is introduced in the very ingenious and interesting work by that author.

The minstrels and joculators of old times seem to exist in the pantaloons and jack-puddings of modern wakes and fairs; many of the same grotesque amusements, and feats of agility that are now practised, were familiar to the Saxons; and the droll holding a pair of bellows by way of fiddle, and using the tongs as a substitute for the bow, as exhibited in the reign of Queen Elizabeth, has a rival in the modern scaramouch playing his accompaniment upon the salt box.

Published by William Miller, Albemarle Street, Jan.y 1, 1805.

N.o 15.

PLATE XI.

THE HALFPENNY-SHOWMAN.

THE great propensity which the inhabitants of Europe have ever evinced for seeing of sights, has induced the ingenious of different ages to invent numberless exhibitions for their amusement: hence the various orders of people may indulge their passions for spectacles and divertisements, from the refinement of the Italian opera to the humble exhibition of the halfpenny show. There have been many modes of entertainment produced within the last century, which have died with their inventors: some of them exhibited much ingenuity. Within recollection, a very curious piece of machinery was shown in the streets of London, the contrivance of a lame journeyman weaver, which represented several groups of puppets; as, a baker, barber, slaughterman felling an ox, washer-woman, &c., busied in their various occupations, and among the rest a very humourous subject, "old women being ground young;" the whole were set in motion by clock-work. The staccata pastorella, also, may be recollected, with a dancing Darby and Joan, the work of a man born blind, who played upon the instrument, and moved the puppets by a spring attached to his foot. We have a living instance of the humour of a travelling tinker, in his having built himself a moveable dwelling in the form of a tea-kettle; and as his family and circumstances increased, adding thereto a new suite of apartments in the shape of a coffee-pot, the spouts of which are converted into chimnies. Thus making every part of His Majesty's dominions his temporary residence, at the same time avoiding the payment of taxes. But the masterpiece of ingenuity in the class of humble exhibitions, is that of Punch, wherein one man has the contrivance to produce a low pantomime, with puppets moved by himself, accompanying the same with the most ludicrous squeaking dialogue that human drollery ever invented.

The subject of this Plate is a travelling halfpenny-showman, many of whom may be seen at country statutes, or fairs. They walk all over England with their exhibitions at their backs.

Published by William Miller, Albemarle Street, Jan.y 1. 1805. No. 12.

PLATE XII.

BREWERS.

IT is supposed that the art of brewing beer from barley was communicated to the inhabitants of this country by the ancient Germans. The earliest notice which is found upon record of the existence of a brewery in London, is in a grant from the Crown, of some grounds adjoining Castle-Baynard, to Robert Fitz-Richard, which were forfeited by the grandson of William the Conquerer. In the year 1295, the reign of Edward the First, a precepe was sent to the Mayor and Sheriffs of London, ordering them to punish corporally all bakers, brewers, and millers, convicted of bad practices. It is likely that this was a thriving trade at an early period, for breweries were indicted as public nuisances in the reign of Edward the Second. The method of making a pleasant drink from barley is said to have been known to the ancient Egyptians. "The town of Pelusium was particularly celebrated for its manufactures of malt-liquor, of which there were two kinds; one, called Carmi, was sweet, and appears to have resembled our sweet and glutinous ales; the other named Zithum, seems to have been analogous to beer." Many ancient barbarous nations are reputed to have made a beverage from a decoction of barley, or some other farinaceous grain; but the art of making a malt-liquor for store, or keeping, was not known till of late years. The addition of hops, or some other bitter, is of modern discovery. Mr. Mungo Park, in his interesting book of Travels into the Interior of Africa, informs us that the Negroes make excellent beer from a species of their corn, by rendering the seeds into malt, nearly in the same manner as barley is malted in England; the flavour of which, he states, resembled our best strong beer.

The British porter, beer, and ales, have the reputation of excelling the malt-liquors of every other country; and are esteemed to be both wholesome and nutritious. Our breweries of the first class are conducted upon a very extensive plan, and afford employment for a great number of men and horses. The machines, coppers, vats, and casks, which have been constructed for the purposes of brewing, as exhibited on some premises, are upon a stupendous scale. One cask, for containing porter, in the brewery of Messrs. Meux and Co. in Liquor-Pond Street, is 65½ feet in diameter, and 25½ feet high; it is composed of 314 staves of English oak, 2½ inches thick; the iron-hoops (of which there are 56) weigh from one ton to three tons each: this amazing vessel will contain twenty thousand barrels of porter. It was four years in building, and cost £10,000.

The brewers were incorporated by Henry the Sixth, in the year 1438, by the name of the Master and Keeper or Wardens, and Commonality of the Mystery or Art of Brewers of the City of London. This charter of incorporation was afterwards confirmed by Edward the Fourth, in the year 1480, with the additional privilege of making by-laws.

Published by William Miller, Albemarle Street, Jan.y 1. 1805.　　　No. 14.

PLATE XIII.

WOMAN CHURNING BUTTER.

THE method of making butter was known at a very early period in the eastern part of the world, as appears by the sacred writings; for among the similies used by Solomon in his book of Proverbs, we find, "surely the churning of milk bringeth forth butter;" and again in Isaiah it is said, in allusion to the promised Messiah, "butter and honey shall he eat, that he may know to refuse the evil and choose the good." It is even supposed to have been in use as early as the time of Abraham.

It is remarked that the Romans did not use butter, except in medicine; we may infer from hence, that these enlightened people were unacquainted with the true method of making it; or during the period when they devoted their minds to the study of multiplying luxuries for the table, this delicious substance, had it been known, would have found its way into their confectionary and pastry. Butter was made about the same time by people of certain countries as a substitute for oil, and burnt in their lamps; particularly by the Christians of Egypt, who used it at their altars: indeed the same custom of burning it in places of worship is said to exist even now in some parts of the East.

The process for converting cream into butter, varies greatly in different parts of the globe. In Barbary, the milk or cream is put into a goat's skin, suspended from one side of the tent to the other, and pressed to and fro in one uniform direction; this quickly occasions the necessary separation of the unctuous and wheyey parts. There are various modes of producing this valuable substance in our own country. In some parts of Devonshire and Somersetshire, butter is made without a churn, the flavour of which is much esteemed; the cream is put into a large metal pan, and stirred with the hand until it becomes butter, which is effected in a short time; this is made of scalded cream. They have also a method of producing clouted or clotted cream; the milk is poured into brass pans, and left to stand for eight hours; it is then put upon a gentle fire, and remains till the cream begins to shrivel; when it is skimmed; having acquired a consistence nearly equal to butter, and is of a cool and delicious flavour.

Butter is generally made in England with the churn; for many ages the pump or upright form was used; but of late years the barrel churn has been adopted, which answers best for large dairies; this machine has recently experienced great improvement. And in some places, where there are very extensive dairies, it is constructed so as to be worked by a horse.

Our trade in butter is very considerable: some compute that 50,000 tons are annually consumed in London, which is chiefly made within fifty miles round the city; 210,000 firkins are said to be sent yearly from Yorkshire, Cambridge, and Suffolk, each firkin containing 56lbs. Utoxeter in Staffordshire is a market famous for good butter; but none is esteemed equal to that which is made in Essex, well known by the name of "Epping butter."

Many excellent laws exist for the regulation of this trade; and to prevent fraud; in the first instance, the coopers are obliged to make the tubs or vessels for packing butter of a specific weight, regulated by the quantity which they are designed to contain. And every maker, before such vessel is offered for sale, shall on the outside of the bottom brand his name and place of residence with a hot iron, together with the weight thereof. And the dairy-man, farmer, or seller of butter packed in these vessels, is obliged also to brand his name and place of abode, upon the outside of the top, and on the bouge or body across two different staves at least, to prevent the butter being taken out and changed, under a penalty for neglect of £5. for each offence. And any person convicted of forging or counerfeiting the name or marks upon a vessel, is subject to a penalty of £40. The city of York, and town of Malton, have special directions it the Act of Parliament for the sale of butter.

Published by William Miller, Albemarle Street, Jan.y 1. 1805.   No. 13.

PLATE XIV.

COAL-HEAVERS.

AMONG the many laborious avocations essential to the support of society in a high state of civilization, perhaps none can be found that demands greater bodily exertion, than the various departments of the coal trade; and the distinctions existing between one rational human being, and another, inhabitants of the same country, and subject to, and protected by the same laws, cannot appear more remote, than by comparing the employment and habits of the collier in the coal-mine, with those of the enlightened consumer of the mineral furnished by his labour. We may consider coal as one of the most valuable productions of this island; for to it we owe the superiority of many of our manufactures, particularly in iron and steel. Hence we discover, that what nature has bountifully bestowed upon one country, is rendered valuable only by the productions of another. The iron of Sweden is principally manufactured in the forges of Britain, and afterwards sent to all parts of the globe. Indeed British coal is esteemed to be so superior to that of other countries for the manufacture of this metal, that many thousand tons are annually exported to different parts of Europe for that purpose.

The sinking of a coal mine may be adduced as an instance of what the daring genius of man will attempt; and the formation of some of the coal works, prove what human abilities can accomplish. Every mechanical power is applied; and stupendous machines and engines are constructed, by the operation of which, a small proportion of coal is made the active cause of raising thousands of tons of the sam; and water acquires the power of preventing the works from being destroyed by its own element.

It is doubted whether coals were used as fuel by the early inhabitants of this country. Ornaments and trinkets were made by the ancient Britons, and by the Romans, of a certain species of this mineral. It is conjectured from the discovery of Roman Antiquities, that pit coal was burnt for some purposes by this people when in England. The discovery of Newcastle coals is stated to have occurred in 1234, and Henry the Third granted a charter to that town for the digging of them. In the year 1306 they were used in such quantities, that a prohibition to burning them in London was issued, occasioned by a complaint made by the nobility and gentry to the King; alleging that the air was infected by a noisome smell, and a thick cloud, from the coals used in the suburbs by brewers, dyers, &c. requiring great fires, to the endangering the health of the inhabitants. Upon which his Majesty issued a proclamation prohibiting coals being burnt in London, and the suburbs, under severe penalties. They were, however, in general use in London in the year 1400; since which time the encouragement to the collieries has encreased in proportion to the destruction of the woods. Many thousands of a hardy race of people are employed in this trade; and our navy is furnished with a great number of its most valuable sailors from the crews who navigate their ships: indeed these vessels, termed colliers, are esteemed the nurseries for British sailors.

The figures represented upon this Plate are denominated Coal-Heavers, and are employed to measure the coals, which are sent to the consumers.

Published by William Miller, Albemarle Street Jan.y 1. 1805.

No. 11.

PLATE XV.

BEADLE OF THE CHURCH.

IT is supposed that the Beadies of the Church owe their origin to the Reformation, and that they were established in imitation of Vergers or Sacristans of the Romish Church. Their principal business is to prevent any riotous behaviour taking place by idle and dissolute people, during the performance of divine service. Formerly, when the lower orders of the community were less civilized than they have been of late years, the office must have exposed them to great personal danger, as many serious riots were committed on the Sabbath; some indeed originated with the higher orders, and in the churches, when notions of precedence were carried even into the holy places.

The decent observance of the Sabbath is of the highest consequence to a Christian state, abstracted of religious obligation; for the morals and manners of a people would soon relax into a dreadful state of wickedness, if every seventh day was allowed to be devoted to the indulgence of idleness and pleasure. Such it proved to be in the reign of James the First, when the licentiousness of the common people had arrived to such a height, that not content with the pursuit of sports and pastimes, immoral, and cruel to a great degree, on the week days, they claimed the privilege of following them on the Lord's day; till at length certain of the clergy, with the aid of the city magistrates, interposed their authority for the suppression of the same. The people were outrageous, and appealed to the King; who, intimidated by by their clamours, weakly condescended to publish a book of sports lawful to be practised on the Sabbath; namely, dancing, archery, leaping, vaulting, may games, whitsun ales, and morris dances; and did command, that no such *honest mirth* or *recreation* should be forbidden to his subjects, on Sundays after evening service; and prohibiting at the same time all "unlawful games; bear-baiting, bull-baiting, interludes, and bowling, by the meaner sort." It is remarkable that many of the Bishops joined the King in this profanation.

May we not look back upon these times without blushing, notwithstanding the zeal of certain worthy men for enforcing a stricter observance of the Sabbath? The good order which generally characterizes the Sunday in this country, is a proof of the highly civilized state of the people; for under the present mild system, there is very little effected by the dread of ecclesiastical censures. Very noble indeed is the conduct of the present pious prelates, who, looking with indulgence upon the inoffensive recreations of the lower orders upon the Sabbath, boldly oppose the irregularities of that class whose rank and education, should preclude the *necessity* of such an interference.

The Beadles of the present time have exchanged the active and dangerous duties of the office, for the more peaceful business of marshalling charity children, or attending upon the vestry. Once in three years the poor children, who are clothed and educated at the expense of the parish, walk in procession, to trace and preserve the boundaries of the same. They are preceded by the Clergyman, the Churchwardens and Beadles; each boy carries a white wand, and being all dressed in the same livery, they make a very pretty and interesting appearance.

Published by William Miller, Albemarle Street, Jan.y 1. 1805.

No. 16.

PLATE XVI.

LORD MAYOR.

THE custom of appointing a civil governor to preside over the city of London is supposed to have originated with the Romans, who having settled its police in imitation of Rome, made it a Prefecture, and annually sent a person of rank, or some one well versed in the law, to govern the same, under the title of Prefect. For several centuries this ancient city was governed by some person of rank, though under different titles; during the Saxon heptarchy, this officer was called Portreve or Provost; after the Norman conquest, the appellation Balivius was substituted; from whence arose Bailiff, two of whom for a certain period governed the city jointly. The title of Mayor was conferred upon the chief magistrate of London by Richard the First, anno 1191. The first Mayor was Henry Fitz-Alwin, Fitz-Liefstane, goldsmith, appointed by the said King, who continued to fill that honourable office from the first year of Richard the First, until the fifteenth of King John. In the tenth year of the latter prince's reign, the city received his letters-patent, granting them liberty and authority yearly to choose themselves a Mayor, which privilege has been continued to the present time, excepting in a few instances, where the Monarch would not sanction their choice; as in the year 1240, the twenty-fifth of Henry the Third: "Gerard Bat was again elected Mayor for that year to come, but the King would not admit him, being charged with taking money of the victuallers in the preceding year." In the fiftieth of the same reign, Thomas Fitz-Richard was sent to the Tower, and Othon, constable of that fortress, was made custos of the City. In the year 1259, C. Hugh Fitz-Ottonis was made custos of London, and constable of the Tower. There were other instances of the City being governed by a custos during the displeasure of the prince.

The authority and privileges of the Lord Mayor are extensive; to enable him to support a consequence suitable to the dignity of his office, a grand establishment is provided by the chamber of the City. He is allowed four domestic attendants, esquires by their office; first, the Sword-bearer, who is permitted to have a handsome table in the Mansion-house. The Common Hunt, who used to keep a kennel of hounds for the recreation of the Mayor, holding the King's charter to hunt in Middlesex, Essex, and Surrey. The Common-Cryer, and the Water-Bailiff.

At the death of the King, the Lord Mayor officiates as the prime person of England. When James the Sixth of Scotland, at the demise of Queen Elizabeth, was invited to fill the British throne, Robert Lee, then Lord Mayor of London, had the honour, in right of his office, to subscribe in the first place, preceding all the great officers of state, and all the nobility. At a coronation, he claims the honour of acting as chief-butler, and bears the King's cup, which custom was allowed the Bailiffs of London prior to the reign of Richard the First; and by an ancient grant he is permitted to wear over his robes a hood of black velvet, which was a badge of a baron of the realm; and a rich collar of gold with a valuable jewel pendant thereon. He holds jurisdiction over a considerable part of the river Thames; and has the power of reprieving condemned criminals tried at the court of gaol-delivery for the city and county of Middlesex. The Lord Mayor is chosen annually by the Liverymen, or members of the several companies within the City, out of the twenty-six aldermen, in which election the senior alderman who hath not been Mayor, usually meets the preference.

Published by William Miller, Albemarle Street, Jan.y 1. 1805.

No. 18.

PLATE XVII.

SERJEANT TRUMPETER.

THE custom of blowing the trumpet on state occasions is of high antiquity. We find this instrument was common to most nations a few centuries after the deluge. The ancient law was promulgated to God's chosen people by sound of trumpet, as well as by the noise of his æthereal cannon. It was used in the Temple to sound the praises of the Highest by the priests, who are supposed to have been skilful performers upon this noble instrument. Until the time of David it appears that no other musical instrument was used in the daily celebration of the religious rites, which was accompanied by a general chorus of the whole people. The Hebrews, in imitation of the Egyptians, from whom they derived most of their arts and sciences, united the occupation of priest and musician in the same person; the sounding of the trumpet was exclusively their office: for even in war this instrument was sounded by the priests. At the siege of Jericho, the seven priests are desired by Joshua to sound the trumpets before the walls of that city; the effect of which animated the army to deeds of heroism, as the sacred characters of the persons who sounded them impressed the soldiers with the belief of their being inspired. An interesting description of the use of these instruments is given in the tenth chapter of the book of Numbers, "And the Lord spake unto Moses, saying, make thee two trumpets of silver: of an whole piece shalt thou make them, for the calling of the assembly, and for the journeying of the camps; and when they shall blow with them all the assembly shall assemble themselves to thee." The blowing with one trumpet was the signal for the princes of the heads of the thousands of Israel to assemble; at the blowing of the first alarm, the eastern camp moved forward; and at the blowing of the second alarm, the southern camp advanced. It is recorded by Josephus that, at the dedication of the Temple, Solomon ordered two hundred thousand trumpets; according to the institution of Moses, also two hundred thousand garments for the Levites who composed the choir; these were furnished with four hundred thousand musical instruments, as harps, psalteries, &c. made of a mixed metal between gold and silver to accompany the voices. Though this account appears too marvellous to obtain credit, yet we are assured that David (who was far exceeded by Solomon in the splendour of his establishment) kept a choir of four thousand Levites. Hence we may infer that Solomon's must have been a stupendous choir. It is said the Grecians acquired the art of blowing the trumpet from the Tirenians, who were taught by the Tirians, near neighbours to the Jews. The Greeks had their trumpeters in Homer's time, for he mentions the trumpet in his poems; yet, according to the author of Pallas Armata, it seems they knew nothing of them at the siege of Troy. The trumpet was sounded by the Romans when they went out to war, and when they were commanded to retire; also when the soldiers were called out to any work or labour imposed upon them, whether it was to fortify themselves with ditch or rampart, or to make their ambulatory or cursory marches; the trumpet ordered the soldiers to move, but not the ensigns, stands, or baggage. They had three classes, "horn-winders, buccinatores, and classicum." The Roman guards were set by sound of trumpet, and were relieved by the sound of the horn. The first account we meet with of the use of the trumpet in England, is in the reign of Offa, king of Mercia, anno 758. From the book of St. Albans, which states, "that in regard of his (Offa's) prerogative, and not of any pride, he first instituted and commanded, that, even in times of peace also, himself and successors in the crown, should, as he passed through any city, have trumpeters going and sounding before them, to show that the person of the king should breed both fear and honour in all which either see him or hear him." This custom is still in existence.

The king's serjeant trumpeters are part of the establishment of the royal household. This band is composed of seventeen persons. The subject of the plate is the deputy serjeant, who is distinguished by a military hat, and wears a collar of silver SS. He commands the men, who wear black caps. The dress is of crimson velvet, richly embroidered with gold lace. Each man bears a silver trumpet, with banners of the arms of England, embroidered, proper, upon crimson velvet. They attend at coronations, royal marriages, and funerals, (when the trumpet banners are black,) at proclamations, installations, and on other state occasions. The serjeant trumpeter holds the ancient privilege of granting licences to all trumpeters, drummers, and fifers within this realm, who, without his consent, cannot sound, beat, or play at or to any opera, play, dumb show, models, rope-dancing; or to mountebanks, prize players, or any other show, plays, or public exhibition or entertainment whatsoever, at or in any of the said places, without incurring the penalty of fine or imprisonment.

Published by William Miller, Albemarle Street, Jany. 1. 1805.

No. 17.

PLATE XVIII.

SLAUGHTERMAN.

FOR many centuries the method of slaughtering animals for the butcher appears to have existed the same as that practised at present; and excepting in Spain and Portugal, the custom seems to have been the same in most European countries: that is of killing the ox by blows of the pole-axe upon the skull, and the sheep and swine by cutting their throat with the knife; there are various representations of slaughtering animals both in painting and sculpture of ancient date that support this opinion. Of late some attempts have been made (dictated by humanity) to introduce the Portuguese method of killing the ox, by stabbing the animal in the vertebræ of the neck, which produces instant death; but custom or prejudice is in favour of the old system, and this is not likely to be adopted. The Jews who reside here have their beasts slaughtered according to the Hebrew custom; a priest attends at the slaughter houses of those who serve that people to cut the throat of the animal. The meat so killed, when exposed for sale in the market, is distinguished by having a leaden label attached to each joint. Anciently the slaughtermen formed one of the corps of the household establishment of noble families, as appears by an extract printed in the Archæologia, entitled, the Slaughterman's Charge, which states that, "he is to receive of the bailiffe or storer, by the direction of the stewarde, all such beaves, muttons, veales, lambes, or kiddes, and those to dresse faire, and clenlie, the oxeskines, and sheepskines, and both of them to be tallied with by the slaughterman. He is to see the tallowe of the oxen, and the suit of the sheepe, be safelie kepte, and to be delivered to the chandler by the weight, and to be tallied for in like sorte as the other; the calves and lambe skinnes be fees to the clarcke of the kittchine, the inmeates, as tonnges, feet, tripes, calves-heades and feete, with lambes heades and purtenancis, are to be called for by the clarcke of the kittchine. He is to keepe his office cleanlie." These must have afforded considerable perquisites, as an amazing number of persons were daily fed by the hospitality of many of the ancient nobility. The following act affords us no very high opinion of the cleanliness of our ancient countrymen. In the reign of Edward the Third, a letter was sent to the mayor and sheriffs of London to prohibit the slaughtering of beasts in the metropolis, in consequence of the plague breaking out in France, and to prevent the revival of it in London—" because by killing of great beasts, &c. from whose putrid blood running down the streets, and the bowels cast into the Thames, the air of the city is very much corrupted and infected." It goes on to state that owing to these filthy habits, the air was rendered so noxious, that to remedy the evil, it was ordained that no animals were to be slaughtered nearer to the city eastward than Stratford, and westward not nearer than Knightsbridge, under the penalties of forfeiting the slaughtered animals, and one year's imprisonment of the butcher. Notwithstanding the metropolis is so much increased both in extent and population at the present time, yet such are our improved habits of cleanliness, that we hear of no complaints of this nature. A curious account of the tricks of butchers of former times may be gathered from a little tract preserved in the British Museum, entitled, an Assize for Butchers, published by order of the King's Privy Council in 1621, which states, that it hath been a thing carefully looked into and provided for by good and ancient laws and orders of this realm, as well as by the opinion of skilful and learned physicians, that butchers should be prohibited from selling any flesh of cattle, which were infected with a disease called the **Noren**: nor to sell the flesh of bulls unbaiten, &c. neither that they should blow the flesh, nor " geld the kidnies of their muttons, veales, or lambes kidnies to deceive the ignorant purchasers thereof, under pain of amercement, and to suffer the judgement of the pillory," with his corrupt flesh to be burnt before his face in the open market place. The subsequent regulation is so sensible that one is induced to wish it were adopted and enforced in every market. No victuels of the city shall give any rude or unfitting language, nor make any clamour upon any man or woman, in the open market, for cheapening of victuals, under pain of three shillings and fourpence.

PLATE XIX.

BRICK-MAKER.

THE art of brick-making is generally said to have been introduced into this country by the Romans, to whom the Britons owed so many of their improvements. Mr. Essex, however, in his learned and valuable remarks upon the antiquity of brick and stone buildings in England, expresses his doubts upon the subject, and supposes that the Britons were acquainted with the manner of making bricks before the Romans settled in England. He is of opinion that this art was communicated to the early inhabitants of this country by the Gauls, who are said to have constructed their dwellings with bricks; and as the Britons held communication with them, and followed the same religion, and many of their customs, thinks it likely that they adopted their method of building. They are supposed also to have made use of unbaked bricks of clay and straw tempered together, and dried in the sun. The Saxons and Normans occasionally made bricks for their buildings to introduce amidst the masonry in the Roman manner: this not being generally known, or attended to, has led many ingenious persons into error on the discovery of ancient ruins, in attributing to the Romans works many centuries posterior to their final departure from this country. How long the English continued to mould large bricks is uncertain, though the form of them began to be altered between the reigns of Henry the First and Edward the Second, when the manner of making them according to the Flemish mode was adopted, which, with little variation in the size, has continued to the present period, but without deviating from their proportions.

According to Pliny, the dimensions of the Roman bricks were one foot and a half in length, and one foot in breadth. Mr. Essex has given the dimensions of the Roman bricks as follows: in the walls of Chesterford some of the bricks were 16 inches and $\frac{5}{10}$ long, by 11 inches $\frac{5}{10}$ broad, and 1 inch and $\frac{3}{4}$ thick; others taken out of the same walls are 17 inches long, by 11 inches and $\frac{3}{4}$ broad, and 1 inch and $\frac{1}{4}$ thick; in the walls of Colchester, the mean measure is 16 inches and $\frac{5}{10}$ long, by 11 inches broad.

The following statement by Mr. Webster, which was laid before the Society of Antiquaries, proves that the Romans held no particular standard for making the bricks used by them in this country. The dimensions of which are at

	Long. inches.	Broad. inches.	Thick. inches.		Long. inches.	Broad. inches.	Thick. inches.
York - -	17	11	$2\frac{1}{2}$	Verolam	18	—	$3\frac{1}{2}$
Ditto - -	8	8	2	———	23	—	3
Kirkstall Abbey	16	8	—	———	12	—	3
Kentchester -	7	7	1	———	16	—	1
Others same place	24	24	3	———	17	—	$1\frac{1}{4}$
Near Ickleton -	$14\frac{1}{2}$	9	—	———	18	—	—
Lincoln - -	12	7	—				

The term brique or brick was given to this useful invention about the time of Henry the Sixth, prior to which period they had been generally termed wall tiles. The taste for erecting large mansions or buildings of consequence with brick was introduced in the reign of Henry the Seventh; St. James's Palace was probably one of the first erected in the metropolis; since which time building with brick has become so general as frequently to be preferred even where stone can be easily procured. The bricks used in building the walls of King's Hall in Cambridge, were sold at 6*s.* the thousand; in the reign of Richard the Second at 6*s.* 8*d.* the thousand: in the reign of Henry the Fourth at 5*s.* $7\frac{3}{4}$*d.* the thousand; in the reign of Henry the Fifth at 6*s.* 8*d.* the thousand.

Brick-making is one of the manufactures in which women and children take an active part: the whole process is very laborious. It is common to meet with a family composed of a father and mother and four or five children of both sexes, from eight years of age to eighteen or twenty, busily employed at the same shed, whose joint labours produce a great deal of money during the season for making bricks, which is from the month of March to the month of September.

Published by William Miller Albemarle Street Jan.y 1. 1805. N.o 20.

PLATE XX.

KNIFE GRINDER.

THERE are few simple pieces of machinery that exhibit more good sense in the general contrivance than the barrow of a travelling knife grinder: these barrows, like most other machines in modern use, have, of late years, received great improvement. We perceive by certain prints which represent the customs of the Flemish, Dutch, and even the French, that the machines used by itinerant knife grinders about a century ago were greatly inferior in mechanical construction to those in present use. In a folio work of etchings, by Watteau, published about that period, there is a picturesque representation of a knife grinder; his machine is of very rude contrivance, having but one stone, and no wheel; to the axis of the stone is fixed the strap which is attached to the treddle, so that the utmost velocity he could give to the wheel could not exceed the motion of his foot by one revolution in an age: the increased velocity caused by the introduction of the wheel to the modern machine, not only spares the labour of the operator, but enables him to perform his work with much greater facility, and superior skill. There is a picturesque diversity in the various machines travelling about the country; some of these are transported all over England by knife grinders, who carry them upon their backs, others are fitted up in a small cart, with a forge, &c. These people frequently unite the brazier with the cutler, or assume the double capacity of knife grinder and tinker. The people of early times are supposed to have been unacquainted with the method of grinding cutlery as practised at present; for in the many representations of domestic employments, &c. that have been met with, painted upon ancient MS. among which are men grinding different instruments, no other machine has been discovered for this purpose than the common grinding stone, such as is used for grinding scythes, carpenter's tools, &c.

Published by William Miller, Albemarle Street, Jan.y 1. 1806.

No. 23.

PLATE XXI.

ALDERMAN.

EALDORMAN or Alderman is a title which originated with our Saxon ancestors, and was bestowed upon the highest officer in the kingdom; it conferred upon the holder of it, a rank between an Earl and a Theyn. He held a jurisdiction over a shire, and was responsible for the persons of those who committed robbery, if he connived at their escape. His power was both civil and military, and he presided with a Bishop at the scire gemot. So much respect was paid to his rank and person, that to draw weapons before him subjected the offender to the heavy fine of a hundred shillings; and to fight before him in a gemot, incurred a fine of one hundred and twenty shillings, besides other punishments. In process of time the power of the Ealdorman was curtailed, and the rank of the title was lost in that of a magistrate, inferior to a mayor. In the time of Edgar, the judges and justices commonly received the appellation of Alderman. Whatever diminution of consequence the title had lost in the reign of Richard the Second, yet the original spirit and feeling of the office was exhibited by the Aldermen, who so firmly seconded William Walworth in support of their Prince, against the rebel Wat Tyler. Nicholas Brember, John Filpot, Robert Laund, Nicholas Twyford, and Adam Francis, Aldermen, received the honour of Knighthood upon the field, together with their illustrious Mayor, for that patriotic service. This office has sometimes been filled by churchmen. The first regular canon in England, who was Prior of Christ Church, in 1108, was made Alderman of Portsoken-ward. Eustacius, another Prior of the same house, not willing to meddle in temporal matters, served the office by deputy, in 1264. And William Rising, Prior of the same, was sworn Alderman of this ward in the first year of Richard the Second. The Priors sat with the Aldermen of the other wards, and rode with them in their cavalcades; but their habit bore the "shape of a spiritual person." It is not known at what period the city of London was divided into wards: Stowe relates that Fitz-Stephen wrote upon the subject more than four hundred years before his time: this city, he states, "even as Rome, is divided into wards; it hath yearly sherriffes insteade of consuls; it hath the dignity of senators in Aldermen." It is known that previous to the time of Henry the Third, the city had been divided into wards, the number of which was twenty-four, and so remained until the time of Richard the Second, when one more was added, by the division of Farringdon-ward; and in the year 1550, the city purchased the liberties of the Borough of Southwark, and termed the same Bridge-ward, which together formed the twenty-six wards, as they exist at present. Each ward is governed by an Alderman, who is chosen by election, and the Lord Mayor is the returning officer. All the Aldermen keep their wardmote for choosing the subordinate officers, and settling the business of the ward; for redressing grievances, and preventing all defaults found therein. Each Alderman is allowed a deputy, to assist in his government; and certain wards, of great extent, allow two deputies to assist their Aldermen. In the year 1692, the city Common Council came to a resolution, that none but freemen, being householders, should have the privilege of voting at the election of an Alderman; and whoever is elected, upon refusing to discharge the duties of the office, is subject to a fine of £500. The office is held for life; and from this body is chosen the Lord Mayor. The privilege of choosing Aldermen was first granted to the city in the year 1240; they were then to be chosen yearly, but that custom did not last long. In 1376, King Edward granted the citizens a charter to elect their Aldermen annually; and expressly declared that they should not be re-elected. Formerly all the Aldermen that had passed the chair, and the three elder Aldermen, who had not arrived at that honour, were by their charter justices of the peace; but, by an additional charter granted to them in the year 1741, every Alderman is empowered to act as a justice of the peace for the city and liberties thereof. The Lord Mayor, Aldermen, and Common Council, compose a government in its nature similar to the great council of the nation; the Lord Mayor, as King, the Aldermen forming the upper, and the Common Council, (as representatives of the people,) the lower house. Other cities and corporate towns have their Aldermen, who are also subject to the Mayor; but their number is not fixed, being regulated by the consequence of the place to which they belong.

Published by William Miller, Albemarle Street, Jan.y 1 1805.

No. 21.

PLATE XXII.

BISHOP.

THE æra when the venerable title of Bishop was first given to the priesthood in Britain, is not clearly ascertained. Former historians place it in the reign of Lucius, the first Christian King in this island, and quote the authority of the venerable Bede. Previous to the fire of London, there was a table in the church of St. Peter, Cornhill, which recorded that Lucius founded the same church to be an archbishop's see, and metropolitan or chief church of this kingdom, and that it so endured the space of four hundred years. Jocelines, of Furnes, in his book of British bishops, has left the names of the first prelates of that see. He mentions that this church of St. Peter was principally built by the aid of Ciran, chief butler to King Lucius. Thean was the first; Eluanus the second, who built a library adjoining the church, and converted "many of the druids (learned men in the Pagan law) to the Christian faith;" Cadar the third; Obinus the fourth; Conan the fifth; Paludius the sixth; Stephen the seventh; Iltute the eighth; Dedwin the ninth; Thedred the tenth; Hillary the eleventh; Guidelium the twelfth; Vodimus the thirteenth, who was slain by the Saxons; and Theanus the fourteenth, who fled with the Britons into Wales about the year 587. Modern historians place little reliance upon these testimonies, and many are disposed to doubt the existence of Lucius, though of late some coins have been discovered that are supposed by the learned in antiquities to bear the impression of his name. There is better authority, however, for believing that this title existed here as early as the third century, for three British bishops signed their names to the proceedings of the council of Arles, Rustitutus, bishop of London; Eborius, bishop of York; and Adelsius, bishop of Lincoln. Whatever progress the Christian religion had made, must have been attended with mighty difficulties, as the Christians were persecuted by the pagan Romans, by their own tyrannical princes, and finally by the Saxons, who expelled Christianity from England.

It was not till the sixth century that its mild influence began to be generally spread under the reign of Ethelbert, King of Kent. To the benevolence of Pope Gregory we owe this event; and the pious zeal of St. Austin and the forty missionaries who accompanied him on this hazardous enterprize, laid the foundation for all the blessings which Great Britain has derived from the introduction of this religion.

Such was the success of their good work, that more than ten thousand persons are said to have arrived at Canterbury in one day, to receive baptism.

During the Saxon government, the right of appointing to bishoprics was vested in the crown, but, in process of time, the clergy were allowed to elect Bishops, when Pope Gregory the Seventh published a bull of excommunication against "all princes who should dare to confer investitures, and all prelates who should venture to receive them." An accommodation of the Popes to the British sovereigns, touching this privilege, began in the reign of Henry the First, and continued varying according to circumstances until the reign of Henry the Eighth; when he tore from the papal power that right which originally belonged to the throne.

When the Popedom had arrogated to itself the right of directing the spiritual concerns of Christendom, ambition soon contrived to blend therewith a mighty grasp of power, and many pages of history are blotted with the crimes of certain of the priesthood. But it is not a generous employment to rake amongst the ashes of the dead to discover fragments of their vices. The pursuit is more grateful to record what we owe to the piety and learning of those who laboured for the holy cause. Not alone to their religious exertions is our veneration confined: the studies of the churchmen kept alive, through many dark ages, those expiring embers of science, that have since burst forth into the full blaze of human intellect.

On the decease of a Bishop, the dean and chapter immediately certify the same to the King; requesting his permission to elect another. The congé d'élire, or usual licence, is sent to them, with a letter missive, nominating the person whom he would have chosen. The nomination must be within twelve days, or his Majesty appoints by his letters-patent whom he pleases. The ceremonies at the installation of a Bishop are solemn and impressive.

There are two archbishoprics and twenty-four bishoprics in England. The Archbishop of Canterbury is primate and metropolitan of all England. Anciently he held primacy over England, Scotland, and Ireland. The Archbishop of York holds the next rank; anciently he held under his province, all the bishoprics of Scotland. The Bishops of England are barons and peers of the realm, and have precedence of all temporal barons under viscounts. They hold many great privileges, some of which are considered almost regal.

Published by William Miller, Albemarle Street, Jany 1. 1805.

No. 22.

PLATE XXIII.

DOCTOR OF CIVIL LAW.

THE creation of this title is generally represented to have originated at Bologna, about the beginning of the twelfth century, and was first conferred upon Bulgarius, a professor of the Roman law. The title of Doctor of Law was shortly afterwards allowed to theological students, at the university of Paris. Some have insisted that this title was held in our universities, centuries before the creation of the Bolognese professor's title; and add, that the venerable Bede was doctor of law of Cambridge; and John Beverley of Oxford, in the eighth century.

The degrees in civil law can only be taken at Oxford and Cambridge; but the college where it is professed is in the city of London. This place, called Doctors' Commons, was purchased by Doctor Henry Harvey, Dean of the Arches in the reign of Charles the Second, where are held the Arches Court of Canterbury; the Prerogative Court of Canterbury; and the High Court of Admiralty of England. All those who are permitted to plead in the Court of Arches must be doctors of the civil law in one of the Universities; who, upon their petition to the Archbishop of Canterbury, having obtained his fiat, are admitted by the judge of this court. The ceremony of admittance is thus: "the two senior advocates in their scarlet robes, with the mace before them, conduct the new member up the court, and present him with a short Latin speech, and the rescript of the Archbishop; then the oaths of allegiance, supremacy, and some others, prescribed in the statute of the Arches, being taken, he is admitted by the judges, and a place and seat in the court are assigned to him, either a dextris or sinistris, which he is always to keep when he pleads."

At Oxford, to be eligible to the degree of Doctor of Laws, according to the strict rules, the candidate must be of seven years standing in the University, when he is admitted to take the degree of bachelor of that faculty, and in five years more of doctor of the same.

At Cambridge the degree of Bachelor of Law may be attained after six years standing; and the doctor's degree five years afterwards. These degrees may be taken, however, in a shorter period by persons possessing great diligence and talents.

The doctors are honoured with purple or scarlet robes; though anciently these colours were only worn by emperors and kings. In England all doctors in the universities, mayors and governors of cities, and the principal judges, are occasionally clothed in scarlet.

Published by William Miller, Albemarle Street, Jan.y 1.1805. No. 24.

PLATE XXIV.

MILK WOMAN.

THE retailing of milk about the streets, is one of the many useful accommodations of our great metropolis. How long it has been practised is not known, but that it was common in the reign of William the Third, we are assured from a description of the customs of London, written in French, and published at the Hague, in 1693. This account states that on the first of May, and the four or five following days, all the young peasants that are accustomed to carry milk to sell in the city, are smartly dressed; they hire a number of vases, and other ornamental vessels of silver, which are formed into a pyramid, enriched with ribands and flowers; this garland is carried upon the head, instead of the milk pail: thus decked out and accompanied by their companions, and a player upon the violin, they dance before the doors of their customers, each of whom makes them a little present. These people at present carry their milk in pewter pails suspended from a yoke, which enables them to bear a greater quantity, and with less labour. The custom of dancing in May is still kept up by the milk people, with this difference, that the garland is much larger, and is carried by two chairmen, as represented in the Plate. In the reign of Henry the Seventh the dairies were kept by women termed milk wives. Stowe has left us an account of a dairy in his time; he says, "near adjoining this abbey, on the south side thereof, was sometime a farm belonging to the said nunnerie (of St. Clare nuns in the Minories), at the which farm I myself have fetched many a half-pennyworth of milk, and never had less than three ale pints for a halfpenny in the summer; nor less than one ale quart in the winter, always hot from the kine, as the same was milked and strained: one Trolop, and afterwards Goodman, were the farmers there: and had thirtie or fortie kine to the pail." If we allow for the adulteration of the milk sold at present, and the difference of measure, three of these ale pints were equal to six of ours, which shews the great increase of this useful article; this half-pennyworth of milk is now sold for four and twenty times that sum.

The London milk carriers are a hardy set of people, their employment being extremely laborious: they attend at the dairiės to milk the cows, from four to six o'clock in the morning throughout the year; and are afterwards employed in retailing it to their customers, from house to house, till near ten. At noon they attend the cow house again; after which they serve their milk-walk till six in the evening.

From a calculation made by Mr. Middleton, and published in his agricultural survey of Middlesex, it appears that the quantity of milk retailed by these people annually, amounts to the sum of £481,666. and that half of this sum is divided in profit amongst the milk sellers.

Some of the cow-keepers are very opulent; one person at Islington possesses between eight and nine hundred cows. The same author has been at the trouble of collecting an account of the number of these useful animals (which are principally of the Holderness breed), kept on the different farms, for the supply of the metropolis, and its neighbourhood.

In Middlesex, Tothill Fields, and Knightsbridge, two hundred and five. Edgware Road, five hundred and fifty. Paddington, Tottenham Court Road, Battle Bridge, Grays Inn Lane, Bagnigge Wells, and Islington, three thousand nine hundred and fifty. Hoxton, one hundred and fifty. Ratcliff, two hundred and five. Mile End, four hundred and six. Limehouse, one hundred and eighty. Poplar, seventy. Bethnal Green, two hundred. Hackney, six hundred. Bromley, one hundred and sixty. Bow, one hundred. Shoreditch and Kingsland, two hundred. Odd cows, two hundred and twenty-four, making together in this county, seven thousand two hundred. In Kent. Deptford, Rotherhithe, Greenland Dock, New Cross, and Bermondsey, six hundred and eighty one. In Surrey. Lambeth, South Lambeth, Kennington Bridge, Cold Harbour, Peckham, Peckham Rye, Newington, and Camberwell, six hundred and nineteen; making upon the whole eight thousand five hundred.

Published by William Miller, Albemarle Street, Jan.ʸ 2. 1805.

No. 26.

PLATE XXV.

FISHERMEN AT A CAPSTAN.

THE capstan at which the group of fishermen are employed, is a simple machine, by which a few hands are enabled to haul a heavy vessel on shore. The boat attached to the rope, is not represented in the picture, as the composition would not allow of its being introduced. The method of performing this necessary labour, is to place pieces of timber, containing grooves to fit the keel, which being greased, admits the vessel to slide thereon, being towed by the rope that winds round the machine. Vessels are by this contrivance, hauled a considerable distance from the water upon a very steep shore. At Folkestone, Worthing, and other fishing towns, whole tiers of herring boats may be seen, thus raised, where they remain perfectly dry, during the months they are not in use.

At some places these machines are constructed on a larger scale, and will allow a great number of hands to work them: such are those at Ramsgate, Portsmouth, Plymouth, &c. by which vessels of several hundred tons are hauled into dock. Capstans are also used on shipboard, for the purpose of weighing anchors; and such is their power when worked by sixty or eighty men, that the head of a large ship could be forced under water, provided neither the anchor nor cable gave way.

The ingenuity of the mechanic has been eminently displayed in the maritime department of most countries; from the simple capstan of the fisherman, to the mighty camel of the Zuyder Zee. This machine was constructed by the Dutch, to enable them to carry their great ships, from the Texel, over the shallows: and such are its powers, that an East Indiaman drawing fifteen feet of water, can be made to draw but eleven feet; and the heaviest ships of war can be so much raised, as to pass with safety the sand banks of the Zuyder Zee. The camel is near one hundred and thirty feet in length, and is made to embrace the lower part of a ship on each side, by the assistance of windlasses, or capstans horizontally placed; upon these ponderous machines the Dutch ships of war were first carried out in the reign of Charles the Second, to meet the English fleet in the North Seas.

Published by William Miller, Albemarle Street, Jan.y 1. 1805

N.o 26.

PLATE XXVI.

KNIGHT OF THE GARTER.

THAT noble emulation which excited persons of mean birth to aspire to rank by deeds of valour and virtue, was wisely created by the Greeks and Romans in the establishment of various orders of merit, which were conferred upon such men as had eminently distinguished themselves in the senate or the field, or who had achieved any other service for the public good. Hence we may trace the origin of Knighthood. Of what passed during the many ages of barbarism that followed the destruction of these mighty kingdoms, little is known: we hear of no custom of this kind till the time of our Arthur; and the interesting accounts of his Knights of the Round Table, are generally considered as the offspring of fiction. That the honours of Knighthood were conferred in the Anglo-Saxon times, is certain; and the Knight usually received his sword from the hands of some dignitary of the church. When Egbert, a Saxon Prince, was recalled to England, to fill the throne of the murdered Brithric, being then at the court of Charlemagne, at parting he received an honour similar to Knighthood; for that great Prince girded him with his own sword, saying, "Your sword, Prince, has honourably served me; take mine, and may it render equal service to you." Many tedious ceremonies were used in early times, previous to a Knight's installation, as watching, fasting, bathing, and consecrating the sword. These rites were observed at the creation of Edward Lord of Brune, in Lincolnshire, who received his sword from the Abbot of St. Edmundsbury. Similar observances were exhibited, as part of the solemnities, at the creation of two hundred and sixty-seven Knights, in the reign of Edward the First. The French, Spaniards, Germans, and other nations, practised the same. The customary badges of Knighthood, from the earliest times, have been the girdle, sword, mantle, and spurs. On placing the belt, the Christian Princes used to kiss the Knight upon the left cheek, saying, "In the name of the Father, and the Son, and of the Holy Ghost, I make you a Knight." The Germans used to add a violent blow on the ear, as an emblem of future hardships. Minshew says, "the Equites, which heretofore followed and accompanied the Emperor, are, in the German tongue, called Knechtes, that is, servitors, or ministers;" but Camden says, "knecht, in Saxon cniht, was in far more ancient times accepted as an honorary title; and, among the old Germans, signified a person armed with spear and lance, as in after times such were, among other nations, adorned with girdle and belt, since called Equites aurati; and sometimes simply Milites." The etymology of Knight is said to be derived from horseman, and is so expressed in Latin, French, Spanish, Italian, high and low Dutch: and in old English they were called Morchog; also Radenknyts. The following ancient lines, printed in Ashmole, carry on the same idea:

Eqves ab Eqvo is said of very right,
And Chevalier is said of Chevalrie,
In which a rider called is a Knight
Arragoners done also specifie
Caballiers through all that Partie
Is name of worship, and so took his 'ginning
Of spurs of gold, and chiefly riding.

The noble order of St. George, usually called Knights of the Garter, is esteemed the most honourable, and the most ancient now in use in Europe. It was founded by Edward the Third, of glorious memory, in 1350. It was instituted 50 years before the French order of St. Michael; 80 years before the order of the Golden-Fleece, 190 years before the established order of St. Andrew of Scotland, and 209 years before the Danish order of the Elephant. This illustrious order is a corporation, held at Windsor, in the castle of which place all the Knights have been installed. It is composed of a Sovereign, who is always to be King of England; and of twenty-five companions, called Knights of the Garter; also a dean, and twelve canons; besides petty canons, vergers, and other inferior officers; and twenty-six poor Knights, who receive (according to ancient usage) a maintenance, as a reward for their prayers. There is also attached to this body, a prelate of the Garter, who must be Bishop of Winchester; a chancellor, who must be Bishop of Salisbury; and a register, who must be Dean of Windsor. Also the principal King at Arms, called Garter; and the Usher of the Garter, who is Usher of the Black-Rod. The dress of this order is extremely rich; and the ceremonies and feasts attached thereto, exhibit almost the only remains of the magnificence of ancient times.

The following list of illustrious foreign titles have been received into the order of the Garter. Eight Emperors, twenty-nine Kings, five Princes of Orange, twenty-four Electors, Dukes, Margraves, and Counts, and two Kings of Scotland.

Published by William Miller, Albemarle Street, Jany 1.1805   N°. 27.

PLATE XXVII.

WATERMAN TO A COACH STAND.

SEVERAL countries have contended for the merit of inventing the useful machine called Coach, but none have been able to establish their claim. Professor Beckman, in his interesting work of "the History of Inventions and Discoveries," has taken great pains to settle this matter; but without success. The first account that can be gathered of the introduction of coaches into England is from Stowe; who complains that the increase of "carres, drayes, carts, and coaches, more than hath been accustomed; the streetes and lanes being streightened must needs be dangerous as daily experience proveth;" he also says "the coachman rides behind his horses tayles, lashes them, and looketh not behind him. The draye-man sitteth and sleepeth on his draye, and letteth his horse lead him home." Coaches were first brought into this country from Germany by Fitz Allen, Earl of Arundel, about the year 1580. It appears, however, that a species of carriage was known here as early as the fourteenth century; for when Richard the Second was first threatened by the rebels of Kent, and was induced to fly from the Tower of London, his mother, being sick, was removed in a wherlicote. The introduction of the side-saddle for ladies, superseded the use of wherlicotes, and chariots, except at coronations and such like spectacles: what the structure or form of these carriages were is not described; but it is not improbable that they might have first suggested the plan for building coaches. The first vehicles of this kind, it is likely, were very rudely formed. It is worthy of remark, that almost every government in Europe opposed the introduction of coaches into their states; wisely predicting a thousand evils that would arise from so effeminate an indulgence. Prohibitions were published, and threats denounced against those who should dare to use them. They loudly declaimed that it would beget dangerous habits of indolence, and destroy that hardy and masculine spirit, which was esteemed the only support of patriotic virtue. Such has ever been the language of half-civilized rulers. Modern history has evinced, that the banner of war is as readily unfurled, and as bravely defended, by those who are nursed in the bosom of elegance and ease, as by the hardy bands of unlettered barbarians. The custom of letting out coaches for hire, according to Beckman, originated with the French, about the year 1650. The projector's name was Nicholas Sauvage, who lived in the street St. Martin, in a house called the Hotel St. Fiacre; hence the name

Fiacres, which the hackney coaches of Paris are called. But it appears by Harrison's History of London, that twenty hackney coaches were used in our city as early as the year 1625. They were not standing in the streets for hire, but were kept at the principal inns ready to call as occasion might require. That they were common ten years afterwards, may be fairly inferred, by a proclamation issued for their suppression, dated the 19th January 1635, which strictly commanded that after the 24th of June next ensuing, no hackney coach should be used in the city of London, nor suburbs thereof; other than by carrying of people to and from their habitations in the country; and that no person should make use of a coach in this city, except such persons as were capable of keeping four able horses, fit for his Majesty's service; which were to be ready when called for, under a severe penalty. Thus it appears that the English used the hackney coach some years before the French; and though this subject may appear of too little importance to contend about, yet there is some satisfaction in claiming our right; particularly when foreigners are not too ready to allow the English nation the merit of original inventions. The advantages derived from the accommodation of these convenient vehicles, are incalculable, as they facilitate the intercourse between thousands of people in this great commercial place every day; and many valuable lives are saved by the shelter which they afford during the inclement seasons of the year. Hackney coaches appear upon the stand for hire, at seven o'clock in the morning in summer, and at eight in winter: twelve hundred are allowed to be kept in London and its vicinity, and each is numbered. The prices of fare are regulated; and no coachman can refuse to carry passengers for any distance short of ten miles, however stormy the weather, or however the horses may be fatigued. A certain number are reserved to relieve those that have been employed during the day, which are called night coaches, and they attend at their stands till sun-rise. Public houses are kept open during the night for the accommodation of the coachmen. The figure represented upon this plate is employed as waterman to the stand, who is licensed, and wears a badge with his number engraved thereon: his business is to feed and water the horses, and to open the door for the passengers, that the driver may remain upon his box: he also has charge of the coaches during the time that the coachmen take their meals.

The office for licensing hackney coaches was erected in the year 1696, under the direction of commissioners; they have a code of regulations, which subjects the drivers to penalties for extortion, carelessuess, rude behaviour, &c. by which the public is much benefitted; as the mode of redress is rendered simple and expeditious.

PLATE XXVIII.

DUSTMAN.

THAT the calamities of plague and pestilence, have arisen from a disregard to the habits of cleanliness, in large and populous towns, the sad experience of former times has too often evinced, of which the cities of London and Westminster have been visited with their share. To prevent the recurrence of these evils, amongst other regulations was the scheme of establishing a regular body of scavengers, and dustmen, the former to sweep the open streets, and cart away the filth, and stagnant dirt; and the latter, to collect from door to door such waste materials as composed the dunghills; for the purpose of preventing the noisome vapours that were used to accumulate in the areas or yards of every house. Happily, since a proper attention has been devoted to this custom, we have not experienced the like awful visitation.

Commissioners were appointed to superintend this business in the year 1670, who were empowered by act of parliament to make a code of regulations for the observance of the public; by which the inhabitants were obliged to see that their servants took care "that the dirt, ashes, or soil, of their houses should be in readiness for the carmen, by setting out the same over night in tubs, boxes, baskets, or other vessels, near and contiguous to their houses." At that period the dustmen gave notice of their being in the streets with their tumbrils or carts, by loudly knocking a wooden clapper, "especially in courts, allies, and other back passages, under pain of the penalty of three shillings and four-pence upon every neglect duly proved.

At present the dustmen announce their coming by the ringing of a bell: they are obliged to collect the rubbish from house to house, which they load their carts with, and convey to the dust hills in the environs of the town. When this custom was first adopted, and for several years after, the contractors received from the different wards in the City, and from the respective parishes or districts in Westminster, considerable sums of money, as a remuneration for the expences incurred, by the number of men, horses, carts, &c. necessarily employed: but time has brought to light, that industry, aided by experiment, can turn every thing to advantage; and that rubbish and filth, the former pests of the city, are now become a source of utility and wealth. The people who perform the duties of scavenger, and dustman, now pay a sum of money for the contract, and for being allowed the exclusive privilege of carting away the rubbish.

Amongst other advantages which the public experience from this custom, must be mentioned, that it furnishes the means of an honest livelihood for a great number of men and women, of the lowest order, who are employed in separating the different materials, which are heaped together upon the dust hills. The sea-coal cinders are picked out and sifted; the largest are sold to the brick-makers to burn in their kilns; the siftings are used as a manure. The rags are picked out and sorted for making various sorts of paper: pieces of rope are laid aside for a coarser kind of paper. The bones are reserved for making ivory black, and various other purposes; and the residue of the rubbish is used for manure, for mending the roads, or is applied to some useful occasion.

Published by William Miller, Albemarle Street, Jany 1.1805.

No. 29.

PLATE XXIX.

LAMP-LIGHTER.

ONE of the improvements of modern police, is the public lighting of streets, in cities and great towns, a custom which the ancients were entirely unacquainted with, though it is now adopted in many parts of Europe. This department is so well conducted in the cities of London and Westminster, as to excite the admiration of all foreigners, on their arrival at the British metropolis. Not only the streets, lanes, courts and alleys, of these great cities, but the roads in every direction leading thereto (and some for several miles), are lighted with lamps, rendering the approach safe and convenient. Before this wise regulation, murders, robberies, riots, and innumerable accidents occurred in the streets, during the obscurity of night. Such was the former state of London, that it was found necessary, upon rebuilding the steeple of Bow-Church, in Cheapside, anno 1512, to erect arches, or bows, to support five lanterns, one at each corner, and one upon the top, for the purpose of bearing lights nightly in the winter, "whereby travellers to the cittie might have the better sight thereof, and not to misse their wayes." The English have a fair claim to the merit of inventing public lights in the streets; for as early as the reign of Henry the Fifth, we find Henry Barton, Mayor of London, "ordained lanthorns with lights to be hanged out on the winter evenings between Hollontide and Candlemasse." Not long after the memorable fire of London, amongst other regulations for the improvement of the City, and in conformity to an act of parliament, it was ordained that "the inhabitants should duly hang, and keep out their candles lighted to the accustomed hour." Notwithstanding the patriotic zeal of the magistrates for the accomplishment of this useful custom, yet so slow is the progress of public improvement, that it was not till the year 1736 that the streets were regularly lighted. One thousand lamps were first set up, but they were shortly augmented to five thousand, in the City and liberties alone; but including Westminster and the suburbs, the number amounted to fifteen thousand. The time which they were used to remain lighted was only seven hundred and fifty hours annually; this was increased to five thousand hours. The act for completing this department, according to the present regulations, was passed in 1744. The lamps are lighted in the streets of London and Westminster every day in the year, at sunset; but those in the environs are generally used but six months in the year,—from September to March. The lamps are all of clear glass, in which are burnt good oil, with cotton wicks; they are trimmed every morning, and are cleaned as often as occasion requires.

The regulation of this business is vested in the hands of commissioners, who are appointed in each parish. The office is considered highly respectable, but without emolument. They grant contracts to particular persons for each district, and appoint surveyors to see that the work is properly performed: they hold committees on certain days, to hear appeals from the parishioners, and to remedy such complaints as are laid before them. The sum for defraying the expences for lamps, lighting, &c. is raised by a rate levied upon the inhabitants, who are housekeepers. The lamp-lighters are employed in the forenoon in trimming and cleaning the lamps, in the evening in lighting them; and they are obliged to take their turns, to go about at midnight to replenish such as are burning out.

Beckman has traced the periods when the custom of lighting streets was first introduced in various cities and towns upon the Continent. In London, as before stated, lanterns were ordered to be hung out, anno 1417. At Paris this custom began in the year 1524. At the Hague, 1553. At Amsterdam, 1669. At Hamburgh, 1675. At Berlin, 1679. At Copenhagen, 1681. At Vienna, 1687, where the lamp-lighters wear an uniform, and are under military discipline. At Hanover, 1696. At Leipzig, 1702. At Dresden, 1705. At Cassel, 1721. At Halle, 1728. At Gottingen, 1735. At Brunswick, 1765. And at Zurich, in 1778.

Published by William Miller, Albemarle Street, Jany. 1. 1805.

N°. 30.

PLATE XXX.

THE PILLORY.

THE ignominious punishment of the pillory has been inflicted upon certain delinquents, even from the time of the Saxons, with whom it is supposed to have originated in our country. Formerly every place that held a leet, or market, was to have a pillory, and tumbril, to punish offenders; and a leet might be forfeited for not taking care to have a pillory.

So much infamy has ever been attached to persons who have suffered exposure on this machine, that they have not been allowed to act as jurors, nor to give evidence as witnesses in any of our courts of law. The pillory was more generally in use in former times than at present. Many crimes that subjected the perpetrator to this disgrace, are now expiated by fine and imprisonment. In the year 1401, a pillory was set up against a prison, called the Tun, in Cornhill, for the punishment of bakers who sold bread contrary to the assize; for millers stealing of corn at the mill; for bawds, scolds, and other offenders. A curious account of the public disgracing of false jurors, is related to have taken place in the reign of Edward the Fourth, for having taken fees in favour of parties at the assizes. They were adjudged by the Mayor of London to ride from Newgate to this pillory, with paper mitres upon their heads, there to stand, and to return to Newgate the same way. Again, in the year 1509, the first of Henry the Eighth, Darby, Smith, and Simpson, ringleaders of false inquests, rode about the city with their faces to the horses' tails, and papers on their heads: they were afterwards lodged in Newgate, in which prison "they died for verie shame." False jurors were sometimes exposed upon tumbrils, accompanied by the ringing of basons, a custom used in banishing them from their ward.

Among the atrocities perpetrated in the year 1378 by the rebels of Suffolk, who were led on by John Wraw, a lewd and infamous priest, is recorded the murder of Sir John Cavendish, Lord Chief Justice of England, whom they beheaded, and as a mark of their hatred to the machine, they placed his head upon the pillory which stood in the market place at St. Edmundsbury. Scarcely less shocking is the affair relating to Sir Patience Ward, Lord Mayor of London in 1681. This upright magistrate, for defending Alderman Pilkington against a false charge, was basely convicted of perjury, by a corrupt jury, partisans of a faction headed by the Duke of York, and was exposed on the pillory.

The punishment of the pillory is very terrible, when surrounded by an enraged multitude. In the year 1756, four men (thief takers), were pilloried for seducing two youths to commit a robbery, and afterwards prosecuting them to obtain the reward. Such was the fury and indignation of the populace, that one of them was killed upon the spot by the blow of a stone, and the others were so dreadfully pelted that two of them died of their wounds in Newgate.

The populace have sometimes been known to sympathise with the person punished in this way. The lower orders of the English are said to possess a ready mode of their own for appreciating the turpitude of the sufferer's crime, and apportion the quantity of pelting accordingly. The perjured informer, who preys upon individuals, finds no mercy; but he whose offence is against the state, is allowed to pass his hour unmolested. When the bookseller who republished the North Briton stood in the pillory in the year 1765, he held a sprig of laurel in his hand, and received the acclamations of more than ten thousand people.

The crimes which are punishable by the pillory, are embezzling of the property of the state, perjury, swindling, and some others mentioned in law books. Witches were formerly doomed to stand on this dread machine; but that troublesome race being extinct; by an act of the ninth year of George the Second, no prosecution, suit, or proceeding can be carried on against any person for witchcraft, sorcery, enchantment, or conjuration in any court whatsoever. Though all pretenders to this art, upon conviction, are to be imprisoned for one year, and are to stand on the pillory openly four times, once each quarter.

Published by William Miller. Albemarle Street. Jan.y 1. 1805.

No. 31

PLATE XXXI.

GUY FAWKES.

ANNUALLY on the Fifth day of November, there is a very general custom for the rabble to burn in effigy Guy Fawkes. To personate this miscreant an old dress is procured, and stuffed with straw, rags, &c. with a barber's block for a head, a bundle of matches stuck in his bosom, and a dark lantern fastened to his gloves; thus equipped, and placed upon a chair between two poles, he is carried about, followed by troops of boys vociferating "Pray remember the fifth of November, gunpowder treason and plot," &c. This noisy procession parade the streets, and beg money of the passengers, to enable them to purchase crackers, squibs, and other fire-works, which at night are played off, after erecting a gibbet, whereon the figure is hung, and kindling a large bonfire to consume the ancient incendiary. This custom has existed exactly two centuries, to commemorate the detection of the most diabolical plot that human wickedness ever devised.

The Gunpowder Plot, as it is termed, was contrived in the reign of James the First, anno 1605, by certain Jesuits, who during the former reign had been devising means to assassinate Queen Elizabeth. But here the conspirators took a bolder field: Percy, a heated zealot, offered (though a pensioner of James) to assassinate his prince; but it was conceived to be of no avail, as the only way to gain the desired object, (the overthrow of the reformed religion,) would be to destroy not only the King, but the Royal Family; and here the mischief was not limited, the whole Parliament were to be sacrificed; and this sacrifice was intended as an offering to the Pope! the father of the Christian church! Gunpowder was the engine destined for their destruction, and a cellar under the Parliament House was converted into a mine, charged with thirty-six barrels of powder, with bars of iron, and massy stones, over which were laid a thousand billets, and five hundred faggots. Barclay has calculated that thirty thousand human beings must have perished by the explosion. This subject is too horrible to dwell upon. Providentially the plot was discovered, and the conspirators were brought to justice, after a long, just, and impartial trial, which reflects honour upon King James, who would not allow of the question by torture. These traitors were found guilty, and executed according to their sentence. Eight of them suffered in the metropolis, four in St. Paul's church-yard on the 30th of January, and four in Old Palace Yard the following day. Their names were Digby, the two Winters, Grant, Rockwood, Keyes, Bates, and Fawkes;* and six were sent to Worcester, and there executed. The others implicated in this treason, upon its discovery, took refuge at Holbeach, in Staffordshire, in the house of Stephen Littleton. The sheriff of Worcestershire, Sir Richard Walsh, with a band of loyal persons, pursued and surrounded the house, which the conspirators had hastily fortified; and the same means which they had devised for the accomplishment of their plot, (gunpowder,) was the cause of their discomfiture, for a bag containing fourteen pounds of that article, which they had with them for their defence, catching fire, they were blown into the hands of their pursuers. Of these traitors Catesby and Percy were killed, and Tresham with Littleton, and some of the before mentioned, were taken and executed.

No conspiracies or insurrections have ever been attended with consequences more direful than those perpetrated under the name of religion, whose all powerful authority has too often directed its blind votaries to the commission of murder, and every abominable crime, quieting their consciences under the blasphemous persuasion of doing all for the honour of God.

The most happy and grateful contrast to these turbulent ages, is opposed by the state of society in England at the present period; when amidst the difference of existing religious tenets, each party cordially respects and wishes peace to the other, and all unite in the same loyal and affectionate sentiments towards the best of Kings.

* Guy Fawkes has been selected for this odium from his having engaged to fire the mine. The dark lantern and matches are in memory of his having been discovered with them in the cellar.

Published by William Miller, Albemarle Street, Jany 1. 1805.

N.º 32.

PLATE XXXII.

ADMIRAL.

THE title of Admiral, as appears by various authors, was not confined originally to commanders of navies. During the wars of the Saracens, Mahomed constituted four governors of the kingdom of these people who were called Admirals, whom he "enjoined to crush all those Arabians that had embraced the Christian religion." Henry of Huntingdon (says Philpot) styles the tyrant of Babylon, the Admiral of that place. Rupert the Monk asserts, that at the siege of Antioch, the son of the King of that city, and twelve Admirals, perished at its siege. And Matthew Paris, in his life of William Rufus, makes mention of one Carboran, "who, after he had marshalled his army, and brought his squadrons into form and order, put those troops under the command of twenty-nine Kings and Admirals."

Marthusias appears to be the first recorded in English history, as holding the chief command of a fleet of ships, in the reign of Edgar; having several subordinate commanders for the regulating of the same, subject to his authority. Some historians state this fleet to have consisted of three thousand six hundred vessels; though others reduce the number to be under one thousand. That the fleets of early times were composed of a great number of vessels, is clear from various authorities. Julius Cæsar invaded Britain with a numerous fleet; and Prince Louis was sent with six hundred ships, by his father, Philip King of France, to assist the Barons against the tyrant King John.

Marthusias was styled Archi Pirata, also Nautarum Princeps, and the subordinate commanders Præfecti. From the time of Edgar to the reign of Henry the Third it seems little is known of this office; but from the reign of the latter to the present period, the register of the succession of Admirals has been preserved. The management of the navy in ancient times was vested in the hands of three Lord Admirals, one for the south, one for the north, and one for the western division. For a long period this authority was consigned to two, one for the north, and one for the west, and afterwards one Lord Admiral had the command of the whole.

It requires no great exertion of faith to believe the accounts which record the great number of vessels brought into action in these early times, as it is probable one of our modern ships of war alone, would destroy a thousand such: indeed the circumstance of a Danish fleet sailing up the river Lea, in the time of the great Alfred, appears sufficient to justify this supposition. That British Admirals have ever been distinguished for their bravery is pretty certain, whatever might have been the size or structure of the vessels they commanded; for as early as the Saxon times we find Edgar held the title of Sovereign of the Seas. And the custom of lowering sail to English ships of war was established by an ordinance made at Hastings, in Sussex, by King John. What the British Admirals have achieved of late years, need not be recorded here; and it is to be presumed that those whose pursuits shall hereafter lead them to enquire into this subject, however remote the period, will find that time has not spread the least obscurity over the naval history of the present age.

The title of Lord High Admiral of England has been laid aside several years; the power which he held is executed by the Lords Commissioners of the Admiralty. We have Admirals of the Red; Admirals of the White; and Admirals of the Blue. There are also Vice and Rear Admirals of each. The Admiral is commander in chief of a fleet, whose ship is distinguished by a flag displayed at his main topmast head. The Vice Admiral commands the second squadron, carrying his flag at the fore topmast head. The Rear Admiral commands the rear and last squadron, and carries his flag at the mizen topmast head.

The figure of the Admiral represented in the annexed plate is dressed in the full uniform, and wears a red ribbon, as a badge of the Order of the Bath, which, with the star and the medal, are symbols of the honours usually conferred by the King upon such Admirals as have eminently distinguished themselves in the service of their country.

Published by William Miller, Albemarle Street, Jan.y 1 1805.   No. 33.

PLATE XXXIII.

RABBIT-WOMAN.

THE inhabitants of this great town are furnished with a thousand articles of convenience by a set of people who carry their stock in trade about the streets; providing them with fish, flesh, fowl, fruit, vegetables, and various other necessaries at their own doors. These itinerant traders are of great use to persons of limited income; for, being obliged to sell for ready money, they are contented with small profit, and their little trading capital is taken to the wholesale markets almost daily, and laid out to renew their stock.

Some of these people carry their goods in baskets upon their heads, others in barrows, on asses, in small carts, &c.; and each has a particular cry denoting what they sell; some of which are very musical, and have most likely been handed down to us as the customs of ancient times. As such we may presume, the crying of hot cross-buns, primroses, ground-ivy, &c.; these airs have afforded hints for several little musical compositions.

The subject annexed is the Rabbit-woman, who also sells wild fowls and pigeons. The rabbits and wild fowl are hung upon the pole, and the pigeons are usually kept in the basket.

Rabbits and pigeons have furnished our tables from early times. In a statute of Richard the Second, a prohibition to taking rabbits in snares was enforced by a penalty of one year's imprisonment. That they were considered as delicacies in the beginning of the fourteenth century, is evident, for we find that at a gorgeous entertainment given by the Prior of St. Austin's, Canterbury, at his installation, to six thousand persons, rabbits were set down at eighteen modern pence each.

Published by William Miller, Albemarle Street, Jan.y 1.1806.   N.o 34

PLATE XXXIV.

JUDGE.

THE administration of the laws in the Anglo-Saxon times lay in the power of the prince; he appointed the Judges and great officers, and could alter the sentence passed on a criminal. It is related of Alfred, that he displaced some Eoldermen for their ignorance, and placed others in their room, who were capable of judging of the laws.

Our first court of law for trying common offences was called Shire Gemote, where the Eolderman sat as president, and the Domesmen sat as judges on the bench; this court was held twice a year. The next was termed the Hundred Court, also Wapon-take, which sat monthly for the arrangement of civil matters. These two courts were highly creditable to the Saxon government.

Soon after the Norman conquest, these courts were done away, and the King's court was established; wherein sat the great officers of the crown, the King's Justices, and the Barons. The King himself occasionally presided, and in his absence, the principal Justiciary. Barons were by the Norman law entitled to hold their courts, for trying causes of a trivial nature; and, as there were different degrees of Barons, and each laid claim to this privilege, these courts were multiplied to the great disadvantage of the common people, who, for a long time, had reason to deplore the loss of their former courts of law. To so great a degree of corruption had the laws arrived in the thirteenth century, that the liberties of the inferior orders were nearly annihilated. Burgesses were treated with the utmost degradation by the haughty nobility, and whole families were bought and sold like cattle at a market.

When we contemplate the distressed state of our ancient countrymen suffering under such unmerited oppression, we cannot too highly venerate the memory of that great prince, Edward the First. No victories could have purchased him such lasting honours, as those he has acquired by the establishment of courts, for the just administration of the laws over every class of his subjects. The courts of King's Bench, Exchequer, and Common Pleas, were completed by him. The circuitous Judge of Assize, and the establishment of Justices of the Peace, were the works of his reign. This prince has been justly honoured by Sir Edward Coke with the title of the "English Justinian."

We have some instances recorded of the spirit evinced by our ancient magistrates in defence of the dignity of their office. Judge Gascoigne, in the the reign of Henry the Fourth, committed the heir apparent of the throne to prison, for an insult offered him, in behalf of one of his dissolute companions. The Mayor of Coventry, in his magisterial capacity, is also said to have committed the same prince for a similar offence. And Judge Jenkins's noble refusal to acknowledge the power of the usurped parliament of Cromwell is equally memorable. This upright and loyal magistrate, when confined in the Tower, and in daily expectation of being hanged, asserted that he would go to execution with the Bible in one hand, and Magna Charter in the other.

An anecdote of the Judges in the thirteenth century, related by Andrews, does not speak much in favour of western plenty or hospitality. They excused themselves to the Lord Chancellor from holding a court of Eyre in Cornwall, "Si veniamus ibidem, macras genas reportabimus;" should we go thither, we should bring back lantern-jaws.

The salaries of the Judges, about the year 1400, were as follows:—The Chief Judge of the King's Bench had fifty marks annually. The Chief Justice of the Common Pleas had three hundred pounds. The Chief Baron had fifty pounds: and the other Judges each one hundred and twenty pounds.

A Judge of the British realm, on his creation, takes an oath of office, that he will serve the King, and indifferently administer justice to all men without respect to persons; that he will take no bribe, give no counsel where he is a party, nor deny right to any, even though the King, by his letters, or express words, command the contrary. And that he may have no temptation to break his oath, he holds his office and a considerable salary for life. Judges are bound to determine according to the known laws and ancient customs of the realm.

Published by William Miller, Albemarle Street, Jan.y 1.1806. Nº 35.

PLATE XXXV.

BARGES.

THAT the advantages of inland navigation were well understood, even at remote periods, may be inferred from the attention which has been paid thereto by various illustrious nations of antiquity. Solomon, amongst other great men, has left a monument of his political wisdom in the stupendous remains of his navigable canals.

The immense saving of expense in conveying heavy articles of commerce, &c. from place to place by water-carriage, has induced a number of public-spirited people of this country, within the last half century, to enter into associations for the purpose of forming navigable canals: immense funds were soon raised to defray the expense of such undertakings; able engineers have been employed; and such has been the perseverance and zeal to accomplish these works, that water has been carried over unequal ground, by raising artificial beds, and channels for subterraneous rivers have been perforated many hundred yards through solid rocks.

In the extensive empire of China, the commercial intercourse is carried on by their navigable canals; so in Holland and Flanders, &c.; and in process of time it is likely, that all the heavy articles of commerce, agriculture, arts, &c. may be transported in Great Britain the same way. The saving of men and horses is not the least advantage of water carriage, as one horse can tow a barge containing as much weight as thirty horses can draw on an ordinary turnpike road, and with more speed. And one man alone will transport, on a navigable canal, as many goods as three men and eighteen horses usually do on common roads.

Cattle conveyed to market in barges, it appears, is a better mode for the proprietors than driving them upon the roads, where, by being worried and fatigued, they lose a great deal of flesh. Armies are transported with greater convenience upon canals, than in waggons; and no mode of conveyance is comparable with this for the sick and wounded, the motion of the barge being almost imperceptible to the passengers.

Those, who place the formation of the first navigable canal in this country to the reign of Henry the First, are not correct. We are assured, that the Danes cut a navigable canal to bring their fleet above the bridge at London, in the year 1016. This canal reached from Rotherhithe to Battersea.

The great labours in this branch of national improvement have been reserved to appear amongst the achievements of the present age; for, excepting the instance of rendering the Thames navigable to Oxford, in the reign of James I. anno 1624, nothing material was done for the improvement of our inland navigation until the year 1715, when the Kennet was made navigable from Reading to Newbury. Since which time, but particularly within the last half century, almost all the great navigable canals have been projected and completed.

The group of barges, represented upon the accompanying plate, belong to the river Thames, and have been selected for their picturesque appearance.

Published by William Miller, Albemarle Street, Jany 1. 1805. No. 36.

PLATE XXXVI.

SPEAKER OF THE HOUSE OF COMMONS.

THE privilege of sending representatives of the people to the parliament had its origin in the reign of Henry the Third. Previous to that memorable epoch, the great council of the nation was composed entirely of the higher orders, no one of inferior rank to a baron having had a voice in the regulations of government.* This council was called by the Anglo-Saxons, Michel Gemot, which in time gave place to the title of Magnatum Conventus, &c.; but after the Norman conquest, the term Parlementum was substituted, according to some authors, in the reign of Henry the First, though others place it in that of Edward the First.

The first writs issued for summoning knights of shires, citizens, and burgesses, bears date the 49th of Henry the Third; though the formation of the House of Commons as a separate body from the Peers, did not occur till the reign of Edward the Third, anno 1343, when, upon a question of peace or war with France, Sir Bartholomew Bergwersh was sent by that King "to desire the Prelates and Barons to consider of it among themselves, also the Knights of Shires and Commons to consult about it in the Painted Chamber;" since which time they have continued their deliberations separately. Anciently the clergy as well as the laity were represented in the Commons, writs being issued to summon two of the clergy for each diocese.

During the minority of Edward the First this body acquired the first step towards that importance which has since distinguished the Lower House of Parliament. To preserve decorum during their debates they appointed a president, and elected from their own body Peter de la Mere to fill that honourable office, under the title of Speaker. It appears that the choice fell upon this person, in consequence of his having distinguished himself by a patriotic opposition to some obnoxious acts of the late King.

At the meeting of a new Parliament, the Commons attend at the bar of the House of Peers, where they are commanded in the King's name to choose a Speaker, who on a future day is presented to the King, sitting upon the throne, surrounded by the Peers in their robes,

* Some antiquaries are of opinion (says a learned author) that long before this period, nothing of moment wherein the lives or estates of the common people of England were concerned, ever passed without their general consent.

When he makes a petition, that the Commons may have during their sitting, first, a free access to his Majesty; secondly, freedom of speech in their own house; thirdly, freedom from arrests.

It is remarkable that this venerable assembly never wore robes, though the Peers have ever been accustomed to wear them. The Speaker alone is distinguished by a robe of black silk, embroidered with gold lace, and is seated in an elevated chair in the centre of the members, to whom every one addresses his speech, uncovered. It is the business of the Speaker to read all bills, or briefs, to put questions, &c.; but he has no vote excepting the house is divided, or the number of votes are equal, in which case he has the casting vote. He is not to interfere on either side, but is to make a fair and impartial statement of the debate. When seated, the sword and mace are constantly placed upon the table before him.

History records some instances wherein the honour of the Commons has been insulted in the person of their Speaker. In the reign of Queen Elizabeth Sir Edward Coke, upon making the usual requests of access to her person, and liberty of speech, she returned for answer by the Lord Keeper, that the Commons "must know what liberty they were entitled to; not a liberty for every one to speak what he listeth, or what cometh in his brain to utter." And on another occasion she charged the same Speaker "upon his allegiance if any such bills were offered absolutely to refuse them a reading, and not so much as permit them to be debated by the members." These acts savoured of the arbitrary violence of her father, who threatened Edward Montague (a popular member of the Commons) with the loss of his head if he did not accomplish the passing of a very obnoxious money bill the next day.

When the base usurper Cromwell abruptly entered the House of Commons with his armed ruffians, to dissolve the Parliament, after turning the Speaker out of the chair, he ordered the sword and mace to be taken away, "as useless baubles."

Published by William Miller, Albemarle Street, Jan.y 1. 1805.

No. 37.

PLATE XXXVII.

PEER OF THE REALM.

THE origin of Nobility in this country has been derived from the King, who, by the ancient feudal law, is considered universal lord of his whole territories, "and that no man possesseth any part thereof, but derived from him either mediately, or immediately." This derivation began by the King's dividing his whole territory into two parts; one to be manured by certain tenants and husbandmen, called socmen, who were deputed to take care of each manor, "and from the profits thereof especially to maintain his hospitality, his court, and estate; having, in every manor, officers and servants for that purpose." These tenants in socage were not liable to be called upon to serve in the wars.

The other part of his territory he divided amongst his military followers, and though these divisions were the least profitable, yet the honour was considered sufficient to induce the chief people to give them the preference, and they were proportioned according to their rank. Provinces were given to Dukes, counties to Earls, castles and signiories to Barons. This disposition was according to feudal law. These persons were called Pares Regni, and were always to hold themselves in readiness to attend the King's person, to defend him and his territories in war, and to counsel and advise him in peace. Hence the origin of our Parliaments.

These Peers divided their estates again, one division amongst their tenants and vassals, and in return received from their socmen, corn, victuals, and provision for hospitality, and all things necessary to their domestical and civil part of life. And another division was allotted amongst their military followers, who were called Knights, and the shares, Knight's fees, "Stipendia militaria."

The degrees of the English Nobility are limited to five: Duke, Marquis, Earl, Viscount, and Baron." These titles are conferred by the King, either by writ or patent, which renders them hereditary. Baronetage is also created by the King, and although the title is hereditary, yet a Baronet does not take rank amongst the British nobility.

Considerable honour and dignity is attached to the British Peerage; Peers having seats by hereditary right in the Upper House of Parliament, being considered as the King's counsellors. Their privileges are also very extensive; they are free from all arrests, unless for treasons, felony, or breach of peace, condemnation of Parliament, or contempt of the King. In criminal causes, they can only be tried by a jury of the Nobility, their peers, who are allowed to give their verdict upon their honour. As witnesses, however, in civil or criminal cases, they are sworn. The laws of England are so careful of the honour, credit, reputation, and persons of Noblemen, that there is a statute on purpose to "hinder all offence, by false reports, whereby any scandal to their persons may arise."

Published by William Miller, Albemarle Street, Jan.y 1. 1805.

No. 38.

PLATE XXXVIII.

WAGGON.

IT is not easy to ascertain at what period waggons were first used in Great Britain. The early inhabitants, we are assured, knew the art of making wheels; but these were applied to their war chariots, and used on open plains. There is no reason to suppose that their heavy articles of commerce, or agriculture, were conveyed on wheeled carriages, but, as with their unenlightened neighbours, either sledges or pack-horses were used for these purposes. It does not appear that waggons were used, even for the armies, as late as the reign of King John, for we have an account of the Barons' horses being loaded with military equipage. On which subject an ancient writer has exercised his wit: "Their baggage horses," says he, "are loaded not with weapons, but with wine; not with lances, but with luncheons; not with battle-axes, but bottles; not with spears, but with spits," &c.

It is probable, that the introduction of waggons followed shortly after the legislature enacted laws for the improvement of the public roads. We find that the lords of the soil were enjoined to widen and improve the roads in the year 1285, in the reign of Edward the First. And Edward the Third, anno 1346, granted a commission for laying a toll upon all sorts of carriages, passing from the Hospital of St. Giles's in the Fields, to the bar of the old Temple. The master of this Hospital and John of London were authorised to take one penny toll upon waggons, whose lading was worth twenty shillings; and one farthing for one horse load of merchandize. It is evident, from the proportion which the horse-load bore to the waggon, that these vehicles held no comparison with the ponderous carriages now used. Indeed the drawings, which represent the waggons of the reign of Queen Elizabeth, show that they were nearly of the proportion of our breaking machines, with the addition of tilts.

The subject of present consideration is a common stage waggon with roller wheels, a late invention, which entitles the proprietors to certain privileges, as these wheels are supposed to render considerable benefit to the roads, by equalizing the ruts, &c.

These waggons will contain a vast quantity of luggage; considerable attention and skill is requisite in the lading of them; and accidents rarely occur, although immense property is conveyed by their means from one great town to another throughout England.

No country but England exhibits such ponderous machines drawn by horses; neither do any other people devote equal attention to the breed of cattle for this purpose. A broad-wheeled waggon, upon a fine road, with eight or ten horses bearing an equal share in the draught, is an object that excites no inconsiderable degree of admiration.

Published by William Miller, Albemarle Street, Jan.y 1.1805.

No. 39.

PLATE XXXIX.

WATERING CART.

WHOEVER has experienced the misery of encountering a storm of dust, upon a highway, crowded with carriages of every description, with horse and foot, in the heat of summer, must acknowledge the great utility of adopting the watering carts; which, after being but very partially used for many years, are at length now employed on the many roads immediately branching from our widely extended metropolis. The proprietors of these carts are engaged by housekeepers and others to water certain districts, the expences of which are defrayed by a voluntary subscription, generally set on foot by some respectable inhabitants, who undertake gratuitously to collect the same from house to house. It is to be lamented, that a rate is not established for this purpose, as a custom so beneficial is equally participated by every inhabitant having houses upon the borders of these roads, at the expence of such public spirited people as subscribe thereto; for to the disgrace of many be it recorded, that certain inhabitants (whose fortunes afford no excuse for such meanness) refuse to subscribe even a small sum for the support of so pleasant and convenient a custom.

The structure of these carriages is simple, but well contrived; the body, which hangs below the axle-tree, contains the water, and the gutter at the bottom of the hinder part is perforated with holes, so placed as to irrigate the road very equally. The watering cart is usually drawn by one horse, but on some roads two horses are applied, when the leader is rode by a boy, and the driver sits on the seat upon the cart. In districts contiguous to ponds, the carts are driven into the water, and are filled very expeditiously; but where they have not this convenience, they are obliged to supply them with water from the pump, which is hard labour for two men.

Published by William Miller, Albemarle Street, Jan.y 1. 1805.

No. 40.

PLATE XL.

THE GRASS ROLLER.

THE study of agriculture as a science, having of late years become a favourite pursuit with the noblest and most enlightened people of our island, has caused almost every mode of improvement to be eagerly sought; and furnishes an additional instance, had it been wanting, to prove how readily the good examples of the higher orders are imitated by the other classes of the community. The recent establishment of societies for the advancement of agriculture, has opened the minds of the most plodding, the most obstinate cultivator; and the husbandry of one county, hitherto almost confined to itself, by the publication of their transactions, has been judiciously transferred to another county, however remote; thus happily diffusing a much more extensive knowledge of this long neglected, though highly important art.

In the culture of pasturage it appears, however, that little general advancement has been made, and the farmer is earnestly recommended by the most able writers upon the subject, to turn his mind to the improvement of his grass lands. The roller (the subject of the adjoining plate,) is particularly noticed, as not being in general use. It is asserted, that those farmers who roll their lands, get their soil more equalized, their grass becomes closer at the roots, and the crop amply pays for the expence of that labour. The pasturage for a considerable distance round London is particularly fine, where the roller is almost generally used; it must be acknowledged, that the facility of getting manure, contributes much to this appearance; but England affords many natural advantages for the culture of grass; and much may be effected by skill and perseverance, where local advantages are not so obvious. The roller is not confined to the grass lands, it is used with success in the culture of grain. Some of these machines are constructed with a cylinder of stone, and others with cast iron; none however accord so well with the picturesque as those rollers which are made entirely of wood.

Published by William Miller, Albemarle Street, Jan.y 1.1805.

No. 41.

PLATE XLI.

GENERAL.

FOR the origin of a captain-general, or leader of an army, we must go back to the first ages of the world; for no sooner had war made its appearance upon the earth, than it became necessary to study the military art; hence every army had its appointed leader. From the first battle fought by four kings against five, in the vale of Siddim, to the present time, has this destructive art been cultivated by men of the greatest abilities in each succeeding age, so that almost every page in the history of the world, records the shedding of human blood in battle.

The qualities which a general or leader of an army should possess, according to ancient notions, are these: "He must be pious towards God, just towards man, and loyal to his master. He must be very affable, very wise, of a sudden and quick apprehension, of a solid judgment, and happy memory. He must be very severe in his command, and yet very merciful. He must be liberal, and free from all manner of avarice; pityful, magnanimous, and couragious; and, in one word, endued with all the moral virtues. He ought to be an old practitioner in the military art, and well experimented in all its parts and duties." To these qualities, Polybius, in his ninth book, requires more, says the author of Pallas Armata, for he will have his general to be both an astrologer and a geometer. That he who is entrusted with the supreme command of armies, should be an accomplished and very extraordinary person will readily be admitted, as he is invested with a command of the most serious nature, the highest honour, and deepest importance, that can be entrusted to the power of any individual, whatever may be his rank; for he is not only entrusted with the lives of his followers in arms, but with the defence perhaps of a whole country, with the dignity of his prince, welfare of the state, including the lives, property, and religion of all the subjects.

The overthrow of an army or armies by his negligence, inadvertency, rashness, or cowardice, may be productive of the loss of the lives or liberties of many thousands, make fathers childless, children fatherless, and bring upon a whole nation the deepest calamity.

The consideration of these things (says Sir James Turner, who wrote upon the military art near one hundred and fifty years ago) moved most of the ancient kings and emperors, and those of later times likewise, to manage their wars, and lead their armies in person.

Those who laid the foundation of the first four monarchies did so, as in the Assyrian, Nimrod, Belus, Ninus, and Semiramis, and when their posterity did it not, their empire was in the wane, and ended with Sardanapalus, who hid himself from the sight of men amongst his women.

Cyrus led his armies himself, so did some of his successors, but when others of them staid at home, and sent their lieutenants abroad, the Persian monarchy decayed, and became a prey to the great Alexander, who managed his wars in person.

Many Roman emperors after Augustus, went to their wars in person, whereby they preserved their imperial dignity; but when others employed their lieutenants (though many of them were great men and victorious), yet the empire was torn in pieces.

The kings of Leon, Navarre, Castile, Portugal, and Arragon, after the destruction of the Gothish monarchy in Spain, went to the field in person, and recovered those kingdoms out of the hands of the Saracens.

When the kings of France of the Merovingian and Carollomannian race kept within their palaces, and suffered the majors thereof to govern their armies, they lost their kingdoms and crowns.

The kings of England and Scotland used mostly to manage their wars themselves.

All the kings and emperors of the Ottoman race went in person to the wars, till Selimus the Second changed the custom, with no advantage to that empire. Since which time we have instances of Charles of Sweden, William Prince of Orange, Frederick of Prussia, &c. leading their armies in person, and with a success that almost excites a wish that it was more general in many parts of Europe. Yet modern experience has shown, unfortunately for the cause in which so many powers have been engaged, that armies have derived little aid from the presence of the sovereign.

Of generals possessing as many of the high qualities, so essential to a commander, as can be united in one person, Britain may with justice boast of having exhibited upon the great theatre of the world her fair proportion.

Published by William Miller, Albemarle Street, Jany 1.1805.   N.º 42.

PLATE XLII.

FISHERMEN.

THE fisheries from very early times have been considered as a valuable branch of British commerce: many ships have been constantly engaged therein, affording employment to a considerable body of men, which, together with the ships employed in the coal trade, furnish the country with its best seamen in time of war. Many celebrated political writers, at various periods, have endeavoured to show, how much benefit would be added to our commercial interests, and to the country at large, if the legislature would give greater encouragement to our fisheries.

An author who wrote upon the subject more than a century ago asserts, that the Dutch employed 12,000 ships and 200,000 men, in catching the fish that frequented our coasts; and that Sir Walter Raleigh made appear to King James the First, that the same people sold yearly of herrings caught upon the British coast, to the value of £1,372,000., besides what they sent to the Straits, Spain, and a great part of France. Sir Josiah Child, who wrote a discourse upon trade about the same period, states that the Dutch gained £5,000,000. annually by our fish; and it is further added, that £10,000,000. have been gained in one year by the Dutch and others by fishing on the coasts of the British isles.

Nature has certainly been bountiful to this country in her supplies of fish of the most useful kinds; we have immense shoals of herrings, mackarel, and pilchards, abundance of whitings, sprats, salmon, cod, haddock, oysters of the finest flavour, lobsters, cray fish, crabs, shrimps, prawns, muscles, cockles, &c. &c. yet notwithstanding these natural advantages, fish, with few exceptions, can only be purchased at the price of luxuries.

Swinden, in his History of Great Yarmouth, has left an interesting account of the fishermen of old. He says, " that from the landing of Cerdic, anno 495, this sand by defluxion of tides, did by little and little, lift its head above the waters; and so in short time after, sundry fishermen, as well of this kingdom, viz. of the Five Ports, (being then the principal fishermen of England,) as also of France, Flanders and the Low Countries, yearly about the feast of St. Michael the Archangel, resorted thither, where they continued in tents made for the purpose, by the space of forty days, about the killing, trimming, salting, and selling of herrings, to all that thither came for that purpose; whereunto did resort the merchants of London, Norwich, and other places, to buy herrings during that season, and then departed." On this spot stands the present town of Great Yarmouth.

In 1292 appears the first instance of protection granted to foreign fishermen by the Kings of England; the Custos of the Eastern seas and the Bailiffs of Yarmouth are directed not to injure the fishers of Holland.

A curious circumstance in the history of epicureism occurs in Hutchinson's Durham; namely, that Anthony Beck, Bishop of that see, who died anno 1310, gave for forty herrings a sum equal to forty pounds.

In 1382, says Andrews, a ceremony was dropped by which a fisherman (supposed to be descended from Edric, one who used that trade in 618,) had a right one day in the year, to sit at table with the Prior of Westminster, and to demand ale and bread of his cellarer: the founder of the family had, it seems, in a stormy night, conveyed St. Peter across the Thames, that he might consecrate the new-built Abbey of Westminster.

Published by William Miller, Albemarle Street, Jan.y 1. 1805.

No. 43.

PLATE XLIII.

BILL-STICKER.

ONE of the innumerable advantages derived from the invention of the art of printing, is the being enabled to advertise the public, by rapid and cheap means, of such things as are essential to be made known, through the medium of printed bills. Before the stupendous discovery of this art, affairs of state were proclaimed to the people by sound of trumpet, or by written notices hung upon certain public places; and inferior matters were published by the common criers, or bell-men.

The prodigious facility given by this invention to certain operations of modern governments, as well as to the general intercourse in extensive and populous states, exhibits a marked instance of our superiority of means for the general improvement of civilization, over those of the most enlightened nations of antiquity.

Within six hours, by the means of printed bills, the inhabitants of a great city can be advertized of a thousand things necessary to be publicly known; and in cases of fugitive robbers, traitors, spies, &c. the Hue and Cry, or notice for their apprehension, is circulated throughout the kingdom in four or five days.

The exertions that characterise the dashing spirit of the times, is visible in the printing of bills; every day some new mode of catching the attention of the passing multitude is resorted to; witness the bills six or eight feet long, stuck upon the walls to announce the exhibitions at our Amphitheatres, Circuses, Schools of Bucephalus, &c. Surely the printers of the nineteenth century have proved that "those who run may read."

But it is to the managers of the lotteries we owe the merit of the Brobdingnagian style of printing; for under their patronage, the letter-founders have reached the *ne plus ultra* of their art, in type of twelve inches diameter; and we have lived to see a £30,000. prize printed thirty thousand times as large as *small pica!*

Published by William Miller, Albemarle Street Jan.y 1, 1805.

No. 44.

PLATE XLIV.

LORD MAYOR'S BARGE.

THE procession upon the water on the Lord Mayor's day is one of the few remaining pageantries so customary in ancient times. Many of the incorporated companies of the City of London keep a state barge, in which the Liverymen assemble annually on the 9th day of November, and attend the Lord Mayor from Black Friar's Bridge up the Thames to Westminster Hall, where he is sworn into office with great solemnity before the Barons of the Exchequer.

These barges are on an extensive scale, are richly ornamented, and covered with flags and streamers, painted emblematically, with the Company's arms, &c.; the rowers wear liveries, with a silver badge on the left arm: thus equipped, with each a band of musicians, they exhibit, moving majestically upon the water, a grand and interesting sight; the Lord Mayor's barge is more magnificent than the rest, and takes precedency in the procession.

It is not ascertained at what period the Lord Mayor's first procession by water originated; the first account of City state barges is mentioned by Robert Fabian, who relates that the Lord Mayor, Aldermen, and Commons of London were invited by Henry the Seventh to the grand Christmas feast held at Westminster Hall, in the ninth year of his reign, when they were sumptuously entertained at dinner, and afterwards invited to a masque, which lasted the whole night. They took water at the Three Cranes Wharf, and did not return until the break of day.

It was customary for princes and the nobility to make excursions upon the water in former ages: we find so far back as the early part of the eleventh century, that King Canute was taking his pleasure on the water, and has left us a specimen of his poetry descriptive thereof, still extant in the archives of Ely! They are Saxon rhymes, and thus rendered—

> " Ely's monks sang cheerfully
> " When Canute the King was passing by.
> " ' Row to the shore, knights,' said the king,
> " And let us hear these churchmen sing."

Froissart, the interesting narrator of his time, mentions his delivering a book to Richard the Second, as he was sailing upon the Thames, bound in crimson velvet, with silver bosses and clasps, and golden roses. The King demanded of him the subject of the book; "D'Amour," answered the author. Richard received the present graciously, and "ordered that he should be well entertained." It is likely this prince amused his parties on these aquatic excursions with the conversation of men of letters; for it is recorded that the poet Gower, being honoured with a place in the state barge of Richard the Second, was desired by him to "booke some new thinge." In conformity to this royal intimation he wrote his Confessio Amantis, which book is sculptured, with two others, upon his tomb, now extant in the church of Saint Mary Overy's, near London Bridge, on the Southwark side of the Thames.

Before the introduction of coaches into this country, it was usual for the princes and other great persons to pass to and fro from the palaces of the Tower, Whitehall, Westminster, Richmond, and Windsor in barges: indeed so many noble persons had their mansions upon the banks of the Thames, that it was highly convenient to them to perform journeys by water.

In the year 1557, the Princess Elizabeth, (afterwards our illustrious Queen,) whilst state prisoner, under the generous and benevolent Sir Thomas Pope, was allowed to pay a visit to her bigotted and jealous sister, Queen Mary, who then kept her court at Richmond. She took water at Somerset Place in the Queen's barge; which was richly hung with garlands of artificial flowers, and covered with a canopy of green sarcenet wrought with branches of eglantine embroidery, and powdered with blossoms of gold. In the barge she was accompanied by Sir Thomas Pope, and four ladies of her chamber. Six boats attended on this procession, filled with her highness's retinue, habited in russet damask and a blue embroidered satin tasseled and spangled with silver, with bonnets of cloth of silver plumed with green feathers. She was received by the Queen in a sumptuous pavilion made in the form of a castle with cloth of gold and purple velvet, in the labyrinth of the gardens; the walls or sides of the pavilion were chequered into compartments, in each of which was alternately a lily in silver, and a pomegranate in gold: here they were entertained at a royal banquet; in which was introduced a *sotteltie* of a pomegranate tree bearing the arms of Spain. There were many minstrels, but no masking or dancing. Before the banquet, the Queen was long in consultation with Sir Thomas Pope. In the evening the Princess with all her company returned as they came to Somerset Place.

Published by William Miller, Albemarle Street, Jany 1. 1805.

N.º 45.

PLATE XLV.

THE ROUND-ABOUT.

AMONGST the many modes of amusement conducted by the low dissolute people who live by attending statues, fairs, &c. may be included that of the round-about, which is a machine addressed to the boys and girls who frequent these noisy scenes. The proprietor charges a halfpenny for each passenger, and some of these vehicles will hold sixty children, who ride for about a minute and a half, being whirled about by miserable straggling boys who receive a few halfpence for pushing it swiftly round, by running within the cross bars that connect it together. There is a great variety of round-abouts, some going horizontally, others vertically, raising people seated in chairs a frightful height: there are also swings of a curious construction, the whole of which in motion together, amidst the other noisy amusements of a fair, produce a scene of the utmost bustle and confusion.

An immense sum is annually expended in this country, in the indulgence of low amusements at statues, fairs, &c. Indeed as many carts, waggons, chaises, caravans and horses, are employed in transporting from one fair to another, strolling players, harlequins, pantaloons, punches, scaramouches, tumblers, salt-box musicians, wild beasts, giants, dwarfs, monsters, learned horses, learned pigs, fire eaters, stone eaters, fortune tellers, conjurors, and fools, as would be sufficient to convey a considerable part of the camp equipage of his Majesty's land forces.

Published by William Miller, Albemarle Street, Jan.y 1. 1805.

No. 46.

PLATE XLVI.

BARON.

THE title of Baron did not originally confer the same dignity as it afterwards attained—that of Peerage, and a seat in Parliament; for the chief burgesses of London were Barons in the reign of Henry the Third, as appears by a manuscript preserved in Guildhall, entitled Laudes Britanniæ, which notices an aid being given by the Barons of London to King Henry the Third, against Lewis King of France.

It appears also (says Andrews) that the higher classes of London were addressed by the title of Barons; for in the speech of Henry Bishop of Winchester to the citizens, in behalf of the Empress Matilda, during her struggle with King Stephen, he begins with, "You Londoners who are usually looked upon as Barons," &c. The merchants of the Cinque Ports of Kent and Sussex had the privilege of this title also, and the representative of these places still holds the title of Baron. The Earl Palatines and Earl Marches of England had also in former times their Barons.

The Barons were anciently termed, "Barons, quase Robur Belle." In the time of war, the safety of the King and of all his people did depend upon their courage, wisdom, conduct, and skill in martial affairs. Those Barons were only accounted peers of the realm that held of the King thirteen knights fees, amounting to four hundred marks, which sum was necessary to qualify a Baron to be summoned to Parliament.

Barons were not considered of much repute in the early part of the reign of Henry the Third, but after the great rebellion that happened in his time was suppressed, such Barons as had distinguished themselves by their loyalty, were called by writ to sit in Parliament: the others, it appears, lost their peerage.

The law of England, says Chamberlain, "contrary to the laws and customs of other countries, calleth none noble under a Baron; so not only all baronets, all sorts of knights, all esquires, and gentlemen, but also the sons of the nobility, are by our laws reckoned amongst the commons of England."

The subject of this Plate is represented in his Coronation robes.

History abounds with romantic accounts of the Barons and Knights of old times: many of the most despotic of whom, aimed at acquiring popularity, by feasting promiscuously all comers, and by indiscriminate acts of charity. A cross that formerly stood in the market place at Sprotborough, which was erected by Sir William Fitzwilliam, who lived about the year 1117, was inscribed with verses, and recorded this custom:

> "Whoso is hongry, and list well eate
> "Let him come to Sprotborough to his meate,
> "And for a night, and for a daye,
> "His horse shall have both corne and haye,
> "An no man shall ask hym where he goeth awaye."

Published by William Miller, Albemarle Street, Jan.y 1.1805.

No. 47.

PLATE XLVII.

BAKER.

THE company of Bakers is considered to be very ancient, though they were not incorporated till about the year 1307. It is remarkable that the followers of this trade are limited to certain profits by the magistrate, the price of bread being regulated by the price of flour; whilst the butcher, cheesemonger, fishmonger, fruiterer, &c. are subject to no such controul, notwithstanding the articles they vend are no less useful than bread.

The titles of the various sorts of bread that were formerly used in this country, were wastel bread, cocket bread, and bread of treat, the same which is now called white, wheaten, and household: also esquires' bread, monks' bread, boys' bread, and servants' bread.

"There was also messengers' bread, given to messengers as a reward for their services; court bread, allowed by the lord for the service of his household; and eleemosynary bread, which was distributed to the poor."

"The peck loaf, according to act of Parliament, is to weigh, when well baked, 17 lb. 6 oz. avoirdupois weight, and the rest in proportion; and every sack of meal or flour is to weigh two hundred weight, and two quarters nett; and from every sack there ought to be made at an average twenty such loaves of bread."

The laws have ever been severe towards bakers: the pillory was introduced here for the punishment of such of them as sold their bread short of weight, or adulterated it.

"In old times (says Stowe) the bakers of bread at Stratford, were allowed to bring daily (except the sabbath and principal feast) diverse long cartes laden with breade, the same being two ounces in the pennie wheate loaf heavier than the penny wheate loafe baked in the Citie, the same to be solde in Cheape, three or four carts standing there, between Gutherans lane, and Fausters lane end, one cart on Cornhill by the conduit, and one other in Grasse-streete."

The same author relates, that in the fourth year of Edward the Second, and in the mayoralty of Richard Riffeham, a baker named John of Stratford, for making bread less than the assize, was with a "fooles whoode on his heade, and loaves of bread about his necke," drawn on a hurdle through the streets of the city.

In the Visions of Pierce Plowman, an ancient book so called, is the following; "there was a careful commune, when no cart came to town with baked bread from Stratford: "tho gan beggers weepe, and workemen were agast, a little this will be thought long in the days of our Dirte, in a drie Auerell a thousand and three hundred, twice thirty and ten."

In the reign of Henry the Eighth it appears that six bakers of Stratford were merced in Guildhall for baking under the appointed assize. Soon after this period the bakers of Stratford left off serving the city.

By the present statues the penalty for making bread short of weight is five shillings for every ounce deficient, and a forfeiture of the bread: such bread being complained of, and weighed before a magistrate within twenty-fours after it is baked, or exposed to sale within the bills of mortality; or within three days in any other place. Bakers are obliged under a penalty to mark their wheaten bread with a large roman W, and their household bread with an H.

Published by William Miller, Albemarle Street

PLATE XLVIII.

WORSTED WINDER.

THE female figure pourtrayed upon the annexed Plate, is employed in winding worsted upon bobbins, preparatory to its being placed upon the loom, to weave into lace.

There are various modes of winding worsted and silk for this purpose, some of which, though very complicated in appearance, are managed with great dexterity, so admirably are the different machines contrived. Indeed, the vast superiority of man's ingenuity over the rest of the creatures inhabiting the earth, is no where more obviously exhibited, than in the construction of the many machines erected in a manufactory for spinning and weaving.

The making of silk and worsted lace is a beautiful branch of weaving, having of late years, attained high perfection. Every colour, pattern, and figure that can be devised is executed by the loom: so that the beautiful ornaments on the Egyptian, Greek, and Etruscan model are worked upon the fringes and laces that ornament the carriages and furniture of the present age.

In the manufactories for weaving lace, employment is given to men, women, and children. The most difficult patterns are worked by the men, amongst whom exists a great diversity of talent; the less complicated designs are wove by the women; and the simplest of all are executed by girls and boys.

Published by William Miller, Albemarle Street, Jan.y 1 1805.

No. 49.

PLATE XLIX.

HIGHLAND SHEPHERD.

AMONG the few remaining instances existing in this island of the simplicity and pastoral habits of early times, may be noticed those of the Highland shepherd, or herdsman, whose robust constitutions, from constant exposure to the vicissitudes of the weather, from infancy to manhood, enables them to brave the "pelting of the pitiless storm." Many a wintry day, and dark and stormy night, do these hardy people pass, wrapped in their cloaks, beneath the covert of a rock, or sometimes entirely exposed, in aiding their flock.

The dog, by being constantly the companion of the Highland shepherd, acquires sagacity, far superior to what is common to the brute creation; appearing to comprehend all his master's commands. Without the services of this faithful and diligent animal, the flocks in the midst of such wild and mountainous regions as they frequent, would soon be dispersed, and perish. The shepherd, who is acquainted with the best spots for pasture, and who watches for prognostics of the weather, manages the flock accordingly, by the aid of the dog, who drives the sheep sometimes to the summit of a mountain, and at other times, to a particular spot upon its side, or into a deep glen, acting by the signals of his master; who stands on a conspicuous height, shouting his directions, and waving his crook, which the intelligent animal comprehends at a surprising distance.

The shepherd at the time of collecting the flock in the evening for the purpose of counting it, fixes his crook in the ground, and stands a few paces therefrom: the dog drives the sheep between the crook and his master, who numbers them as they pass; but if a straggler goes on the outside, and mixes with those who have passed muster, the dog immediately pursues, singles him out, and brings him back.

The hardiest of the flocks are known in the cold and stormy season, by their feeding on the highest and most exposed parts of a mountain; whilst those who are less healthy and strong, pick their food under shelter of its sides, and in a lower region.

These herdsmen are at a certain season of the year employed to drive their cattle and sheep, from the northern parts of Scotland to the western, and other parts of England, and like the shepherds of old, move onwards during the night, by their observation of the stars.

The dress of the Highland shepherd is ancient and very picturesque; the appendages to which are a pouch for the oatmeal or oat cakes, a mull made of a ram's horn to contain snuff, with a little spoon attached thereto: and a dirk by their side.

Published by William Miller Albemarle Street, Jan.ʸ 1. 1806.

N°. 50

PLATE L.

PRISON SHIPS.

THE prison ships represented in the annexed plate, are stationed off the Tower of London, and are fitted up to receive impressed seamen for manning the navy; these vessels are called Tenders.

The impressing seamen for the service of the state is, according to Blackstone, of ancient date; though there is no existing law that authorises the practice. Nothing can be more distressing than to reflect, that the brave fellows who are idolized by the country, should be liable, through state necessity, to be torn from their homes, when every other subject of his Majesty, in this country, so justly renowned for its liberty, has his personal safety protected by the laws. Nothing could be done by the legislature in the way of reform perhaps, more grateful to the feelings of the people, than the doing away the practice of impressing seamen.

It is some consolation, however, to know that these vessels, instead of being what they were some years ago, the most loathsome and filthy of prisons, too often governed by unfeeling and relentless miscreants, are now preserved clean and healthy; and every humane attention, that can tend to soothe the unfortunate prisoners, is administered by the persons who have them in charge.

Published by William Miller, Albemarle Street, Jan.y 1 1808. No. 51.

PLATE LI..

LORD MAYOR'S STATE COACH.

ON the morning of the ninth of November, on which day the Lord Mayor of the City of London enters upon his office, the Aldermen and Sheriffs meet at the Mansion House, from whence they attend him to Guildhall in a procession formed by coaches; and at noon go on to the Three Cranes Stairs, where the Lord Mayor, Aldermen, Recorder, and Sheriffs are attended by several corporations of the citizens in their robes, who embark in magnificent barges to proceed to Westminster, as described in another part of this Work. When the ceremony is ended at Westminster, they return to Blackfriars Bridge, from whence the livery of many of the City companies march to their respective stands, for this occasion erected on both sides of the streets through which his Lordship has to pass.

The Lord Mayor being landed, a procession commences, which is more splendid than what is seen on any other public occasion: first, the Artillery company marching with flags, trumpets, &c.; then the company of which the Lord Mayor is a member; then follows several others, with music, flags, and streamers, bearing devices of the mysteries of their trades, arms, &c., amongst whom the armourers make a conspicuous and interesting part, having on horseback a man completely equipped in bright armour, and two others attired with breast plates, shoulder pieces, and helmets; the next in the procession are the Lord Mayor's trumpeters in scarlet cloaks, and the six state footmen in their splendid liveries, followed by the state coach drawn by six horses richly caparisoned and dressed with ribbons, together with the Aldermen, Recorder, Sheriffs, Chamberlain, Common Serjeant, Town Clerk, &c. in their several coaches and chariots, proceeding in this manner to Guildhall, where a grand feast is provided; and each Company is entertained at its respective hall on the same day.

The splendor of a Lord Mayor's feast has impressed strangers, and particularly foreign ambassadors, with high notions of the riches and hospitality of the City of London: several of our Kings have been entertained at Guildhall with feasts truly princely.

Many of the most splendid pagentries and feasts, that we find recorded in the history of this country, have been made at the expense of the citizens of London. Amongst many other illustrious persons that they have had the honour of entertaining was Edward the Black Prince, on his entrance into London with his royal prisoner, John

King of France, who was taken at the celebrated battle of Poictiers. It is thus described: "When they came to Southwark they were met by upwards of a thousand of the citizens of London on horseback, dressed in a superb manner; and by a prodigious concourse of people on foot. The captive monarch was clad in royal apparel, and mounted on a white courser, remarkable for its size and beauty, while the victorious prince rode by his side, on a little black horse in ordinary trappings. When they arrived at the foot of London Bridge, they were received by the Mayor, Aldermen, and Sheriffs, and the several city companies, dressed in their formalities, and attended by stately pageants.

"In this manner they were conducted through the streets of London, which were decorated with the richest tapestries, whilst the citizens exhibited to public view their plate, silks, and other furniture, as a proof of their riches: and as a testimony of their warlike genius, they exposed in the balconies and shop windows an incredible number of bows, arrows, helmets, shields, croslets, breast and back pieces, coats of mail, gauntlets, vambraces, swords, spears, battle-axes, harness for horses, and other military accoutrements.

"The cavalcade was so numerous, and the concourse of people assembled to behold it so prodigious, that it continued from three o'clock in the morning until noon, when the victorious prince presented the King of France to his father, who received him with the utmost politeness."

And in the year 1363, Henry Picards, who had passed his mayoralty, had the honour to entertain with a feast four monarchs, King Edward the Third, the King of Scotland, King of France, and the King of Cyprus, besides Edward Prince of Wales, and most of the principal nobility of the kingdom.

PLATE LII.

SMITHFIELD DROVER.

A CONSIDERABLE number of men and boys are employed as drovers, whose business is to attend the great cattle market, which is held for the sale of bulls, cows, oxen, sheep, calves, and pigs, in Smithfield every Monday and Friday throughout the year. The cattle, sheep, &c. after resting at Islington and its neighbourhood on Thursday, are driven to Smithfield by these people, the whole of that night previous to the Friday's market, and also during the Sunday night preceding the Monday's market. They are also engaged the whole time of the two market days in driving the cattle, sheep, &c. purchased by the butchers, to the different parts of the metropolis and adjacent parts.

By a wise and humane regulation adopted during the mayoralty of Alderman Newman, a few years since, each drover is obliged, under a penalty, to wear a badge bearing his number, upon the left arm; in consequence whereof a great deal of barbarous usage which the devoted animals were subject to, at the hands of their merciless and capricious drivers, is in great measure done away; as the drovers are thereby laid open to information, and severely punished for treating the animals committed to their charge with wanton cruelty.

Smithfield has been used as a market for the sale of cattle, sheep, horses, &c. for many ages. Fitzstephen, a monk of Canterbury, who wrote in the reign of Henry the Second, has left a description thereof written in Latin, as it appeared in his time, which has been thus translated: "Without one of the gates is a certain field, plain (or smooth) both in name and situation. Every Friday, except some greater festival come in the way, there is a fine sight of good horses to be sold: many come out of the city to buy or look on, to wit, earls, barons, knights, citizens, all resorting thither. It is a pleasant sight there to behold the animals, well fleshed, sleek, and shining, delightfully walking, and their feet on either side up and down together by turns: or else trotting horses, which are more convenient for men that bear arms; these, although they set a little harder, go away readily, and lift up and set down together the contrary feet on each side. Here are also young colts of good breed, that have not been well accustomed to the bridle; these flying about, and by mounting bravely shew their mettle. Here are principal horses, strong and well limbed. Here also are breast horses, fit to be joined by couples, very fair and handsome, and sleek about the ears, carrying their necks aloft, being well fleshed, and round about the buttocks. In another part stand the country people with cattle and commodities of the field, large swine, and kine with their udders strutting out, fair bodied oxen, and the woolley flock."

Published by William Miller, Albemarle Street, Jany 1.1805.

No. 53.

PLATE LIII.

DRAGOON.

IT is not known how long the science of war had been cultivated before armed men fought on horseback, for the most important events of every kind, as well as great battles, are related in sacred history with remarkable brevity.

It appears the Egyptians had a numerous cavalry; for besides the six hundred chariots which were employed by Pharaoh in pursuit of the Israelites, we may add two hundred thousand foot, and fifty thousand horse, if the testimony of Josephus may be taken in addition to the account of Moses.

The Greeks, Romans, and some other historians, have transmitted accounts of their cavalry; and it appears that few nations have made war without horse, as well as foot soldiers.

Amongst the ancient Romans, and in many other nations, till within the last three hundred years, the cavalry was considered as a more noble service than the foot; the men at arms or curiassiers particularly, were all gentlemen, and most of them were of high extraction. Sir James Turner writes, that when the Romans said a man was *equestris ordinis*, they meant he was a gentleman; and when they spoke so, it inferred that he was of that rank, or class, out of which horsemen were chosen to serve in the wars. This made them demand as their right, the precedency of the foot.

It seems there were no regiments of horse till about two centuries ago; they were in troops or companies, varying in number, some being composed of two hundred, others one hundred, and some even less; these were upon occasions of service joined together, but were not called a regiment, nor had the commander thereof the title of colonel.

In almost every country, and in every age, the greatest consideration has been devoted to the displaying of military pomp, and human ingenuity has been equally exerted by the enlightened Grecian armourer, and the unenlightened savage: the helmet and shield of Achilles were not more carefully wrought, than the tomahawk and target of the Indian chief.

An interesting account of the army marshalled under Henry the Second of France, written by an anonymous author of that age, relates that, "His cavalry was divided into Gens-d'Arms, Archers, Light Horsemen, and Harquebusiers: His Cuirassiers or Gens-d'Arms, consisting all of persons of noble families, were about one thousand, admirably well mounted on French coursers, Turkey horses, or Spanish gennets. They were strongly armed for the defensive; for offence, they had each a lance, a mace, and a sword. Their horses were armed with bards and plates of brass, richly caparisoned; and many other horses they had, on which (besides their led horses) their servants, pages and grooms rode. The captains and other officers of these Gens-d'Arms were in rich armour gilded and curiously wrought; they were mounted on courageous horses, who were armed and richly caparisoned, and their harness covered with either velvet, or cloth of tissue, with goldsmith work, or embroidery. Every one of these Gens-d'Arms had an Archer, who followed him, by the French constitutions of war, who though they then used neither bow nor arrow (as formerly they did), yet did still retain the name of Archers. They rode on small but very nimble horses, who vaulted pleasantly: each of them carried a lance, a pistol, and a sword, all of them well accoutred, striving who should appear finest. The Light Horsemen were mounted on good nags, little, but very swift; for armour they had light helmets, corslets, and sleeves; for offensive arms, each of them had a cutlace, and either a half lance, or a pistol, which of them he pleased, but not both. Of these horse there were about eighteen hundred. The Harquebusiers were mounted on as good gelding as they could make themselves masters of; they had jacks, morrions, and sleeves of mail for their defence; their weapons were swords, and harquebusses of three feet long, hanging at the courches of their saddles. He had about fifteen hundred of them.

"Besides all these there were about four hundred English gentlemen, all volunteers, under the command of an English Lord; they were mounted on handsome and swift geldings; they were provided with little armour for defence; their weapons were swords and lances, like half pikes. These were King Henry's forces."

The subject of the annexed plate is an officer of the Tenth, or Prince of Wales's Dragoons.

Published by William Miller Albemarle Street, Jany 1, 1805.   N.º 54.

PLATE LIV.

ROYAL MAIL.

THE improvement on the invention of the Post, by the introduction of Mail Coaches, was entirely planned by John Palmer, Esq. Comptroller General of the Post Office.

In the memorial laid by that gentleman before Mr. Pitt, he says, "The post at present, instead of being the swiftest, is almost the slowest conveyance in this country; and though from the great improvement in the roads, other carriers have proportionably mended their speed, the post is as slow as ever. It is likewise very unsafe, as the frequent robberies of it testify; and to avoid a loss of this nature, people generally cut Bank bills, or bills at sight, in two, and send the parts by different posts."

The Postmasters General advertised directions to the public how to divide a bill, in such a manner as to prevent its being of any use to a robber. Rewards were also repeatedly held out for the best constructed mail cart, to frustrate the attack of the plunderer, but without effect. The mails were generally entrusted to some very low or worthless boy, mounted on a miserable hack, incapable of flight, who was unequal to its defence, and too often suspected to be in collusion with the robber.

Previous to this establishment, the diligence that sat out from Bath at four or five on Monday afternoon, would deliver a letter about ten on Tuesday morning: while the post that left the same place five or six hours after, did not deliver a letter till two or three on Wednesday afternoon, and frequently much later. This instance is adduced as the general, or average, rate of loss of time. In consequence of which numberless letters were sent by diligences, for safety and for speed, though paid for as parcels; and the revenue of the Post Office materially injured thereby.

To obviate these impediments, Mr. Palmer proposed to Government to employ the diligences as a means of conveyance for letters, allowing so much per mile to the proprietors thereof. Many of these carriages were constructed for this purpose on an improved plan, and were called mail coaches: they are protected by the coachman and a guard, armed with a blunderbuss and brace of pistols each.

The mail coaches are obliged to be very punctual to the time fixed at their different stages; and a master at every inn where the horses change, is obliged under a penalty, to be ready with his packet of letters to deliver to the guard, (who puts them in a general bag,) and to receive those brought for his district. And so peremptory are the orders for the coachman's punctuality, that if the bags are not in readiness at the inns or other appointed places, the mails are not to wait.

To the credit of Mr. Palmer, it should be mentioned, that the contracts for the conveyance of letters are at £20,000. per annum less than the sum agreed for in his plan. The acceleration and extension of the posts are also far greater than were at first promised, the mails being now conveyed not only in half the time they used to be, to most parts of the kingdom, but in one-third, and even one fourth of the time in many of the cross posts: these posts are likewise made daily, instead of three days per week to 320 towns; and also the same additional convenience given to 201 towns in the general posts.

The coachmen and guards wear the Royal livery, and on the anniversary of the King's birth-day, the mail coaches drive along Pall-Mall before the King's Palace, and up St. James's Street; on which day the coaches are newly painted, the horses are caparisoned with ribands, and the coachmen and guards appear in their new dresses. This procession exhibits such a shew of fine blood horses, as no other country ever employed for the service of public stage coaches.

Published by William Miller, Albemarle Street, Jan.y 1. 1805.   N.o 55

PLATE LV.

LIFE-BOAT.

THE meritorious invention of the life-boat owes it origin to a circumstance highly creditable to Sir Cuthbert Heron, Bart. of South Shields, who in the year 1789, on seeing the ship Adventure in great distress on the Herd Sands, offered a reward to any seaman who would venture out to her assistance; and though the mariners of that neighbourhood are a bold and hardy race, none would put off; the ship was wrecked within three hundred yards of the shore, and the unfortunate crew perished in sight of a crowded beach.

This gave rise to a meeting of the gentleman of South Shields, who offered a reward to any person who should deliver to them a plan of a boat, that should be capable of going off to distressed ships in heavy gales, and bring the crews to shore. Amongst the candidates for the proffered reward was Mr. Henry Greathead, whose model being approved of, a committee was appointed, and a subscription raised for the building a boat upon his plan.

The boat being completed, there was some difficulty in procuring sailors to venture on so daring an enterprize, as launching upon a tremendous sea in an open boat; but stimulated by a reward, the boat at length was launched, and the crew of a stranded vessel, by its means, was brought in safety to the shore. This success on the first trial established its utility, and the boat has since been readily manned, and happily on every occasion has its efforts been attended with success.

Amongst numerous instances of its great superiority over other boats on such dangerous service, is noticed that on January 1, 1795: "The ship Parthenius of Newcastle was driven on the Herd Sand; the life-boat went to her assistance; when the sea breaking over the ship as the boat was ranging alongside, the boat was so violently shaken, that her bottom was actually hanging loose: under these circumstances, she went three times off to the ship, without being affected by the water in her."

The account of Captain William Carter of Newcastle states, that on the 28th of November, 1797, the ship Planter of London was driven on shore near Tynemouth Bar, by the violence of a gale; the life-boat came out, and took fifteen persons from the ship, which the boat had scarcely quitted, before the ship went to pieces; that without the boat, they must all have inevitably perished, as the wreck came on shore soon after the life-boat. The ships Gateshead and Mary of Newcastle, the Beaver of North Shields, and a sloop, were in the same situation with the Planter. The crew of the Gateshead, nine in number, took to their own boat, which foundered, and seven of them were lost; the other two saved themselves by ropes thrown from the Mary. After the life-boat had landed the crew of the Planter, she went off successively to the other vessels, and brought the whole of their crews safe to the shore, together with the two persons saved from the boat of the Gateshead. Mr. Carter adds, that he has seen the life-boat go to the assistance of other vessels at different times, and that she ever succeeded in bringing the crews on shore; that he had several times seen her come on shore full of water, and always safe.

The Duke of Northumberland interested himself much in behalf of the inventor of the life-boat, and wrote to the Society for the Encouragement of Arts, Manufactures, and Commerce, in testimony of its utility, when a model thereof was submitted to the inspection of a committee of that patriotic and highly respectable body. This nobleman had a life-boat built at his expence, and presented it to the town of North Shields, attaching an annuity thereto for its support; which boat has saved many valuable seamen from a watery grave.

Mr. Greathead has received several honorary rewards for his invention. Fifty pounds was awarded from the Society abovementioned: since which twelve hundred pounds have been voted to him by Parliament; and he has also received rewards from the Trinity House, and the Members at Lloyds.

Published by William Miller, Albemarle Street, Jany 1 1805.

N.º 56.

PLATE LVI.

ROYAL STATE CARRIAGE.

THE royal state coach is used by his Majesty in going to and from St. James's Palace to the Parliament House, at the opening and closing of the Sessions. In his train are the state carriages of the Prince of Wales, Duke of York, Lord Chancellor, Master of the Horse, &c. The procession, which is very splendid, the royal carriage being drawn by eight cream-coloured horses, and the others by six horses each, is preceded by the King's serjeant trumpeters; and the King's coach is attended by the royal footmen, in scarlet dresses, richly embroidered with gold, who have black caps upon their heads, and canes in their hands, walking four on each side, and a group of them standing upon the hinder part of the carriage; and is guarded by the band of yeomen of the body guard, and the Royal Horse Guards.

This coach was built for our present beloved Sovereign soon after his ascending the throne. The carriage of the coach is composed of four tritons, who support the body with cables fastened to the roots of their fins: the two placed on the front of the carriage bear the driver on their shoulders, and are represented in the action of sounding their shells to announce the approach of the monarch of the sea. This allegory all nations must allow to have been prophetic. Those on the back part carry the imperial fasces, topt with tridents instead of the ancient axes: the driver's foot board is a large scollop-shell supported by bunches of reeds and other marine plants; the pole represents a bundle of lances, and the wheels are imitated from those of the ancient triumphal chariots. The body of the coach is composed of eight palm trees, which branching out at the top, sustain the roof; the four angular trees are loaded with trophies, allusive to the victories obtained by Britain over her enemies. On the centre of the roof stand three boys, the genii of England, Scotland, and Ireland, supporting on their heads the imperial crown, and holding in their hands the sceptre, sword of state, and ensigns of knighthood: their bodies are adorned with festoons of laurel, which fall from thence to the four corners of the roof. The intervals between the palm trees, which form the body of the coach, are filled in the upper part with plates of glass, and below with panels adorned with painting. On the first panel is represented Britannia seated on a throne, holding in her hand a staff of liberty, attended by Religion, Justice, Wisdom, Valour, Fortitude, and Victory presenting her with a garland of laurel. On the back panel, Neptune issuing from his palace, drawn by sea horses, and attended by the Winds, the Rivers, Tritons, Naiads, &c. bringing the tribute of the world to the British shore. On one of the doors is represented Mars, Minerva, and Mercury supporitng the imperial crown of Britain, and on the other, Industry, and Ingenuity giving a cornucopia to the Genius of England. The other four panels represent the liberal arts and sciences protected; History recording the reports of Fame; and Peace burning the implements of War. The inside of the coach is lined with crimson velvet richly embroidered with gold. All the wood work is triple gilt, and all the painting highly varnished. The harness is of deep red morocco leather, the reins of crimson silk, and the clothes, saddles, &c. of crimson velvet, embroidered with gold; the buckles and ornaments, &c. of the whole harness is gilt, and are extremely rich, and well designed.

The expences for building the state coach were,

	£.	s.	d.
Coach-maker	1673	15	0
Carver	2500	0	0
Gilder	933	14	0
Painter	315	0	0
Laceman	737	10	7
Chaser	665	4	6
Harness-maker	385	15	0
Mercer	202	5	10½
Bit-maker	99	6	6
Milliner	31	3	4
Sadler	101	6	6
Woollen-Draper	4	3	6
Cover-maker	3	2	6
	£7,562	4	3½

The first person recorded to have rode in a coach with six horses in this country, was the Duke of Buckingham, anno 1616, the unworthy favourite of two kings: to ridicule this pomp the Earl of Northumberland put eight horses to his carriage. The first carriage suspended upon springs was adopted by Lewis the Fourteenth. A splendid carriage was used by the first wife of the Emperor Leopold, which cost 38,000 florins. The Emperor's imperial coaches, says Beckman, near two centuries ago, were covered over with red cloth and black nails, the harness was black, and in the work there was no gold; the panels were of glass. These coaches had leather traces, but the ladies in the imperial suite were obliged to be contented with carriages, the traces of which were made with ropes.

At the magnificent court of the Duke Ernest Augustus of Hanover, says the same author, there were in the year 1681, fifty gilt coaches with six horses each; so early did Hanover begin to surpass other cities in the number of its carriages.

Published by William Miller, Albemarle Street, Jan.y 1. 1805.

N.o 57.

PLATE LVII.

LOTTERY WHEEL.

THE English lottery originated in the reign of Queen Elizabeth, anno 1569, and was established for the purpose of raising a sum of money to defray part of the expences incurred in repairing the havens. There were 40,000 tickets in this lottery, and the holder of a prize was entitled to certain articles of plate.

In the year 1612, and in the reign of James the First, this plan for raising money was resorted to again, with a temptation suited to the occasion, in a prize of plate to the amount of 4,000 crowns. These lotteries were publicly drawn, both day and night, at the west door of St. Paul's cathedral.

Such was considered the pernicious tendency of this extensive mode of gambling, that an act of William and Mary declared all lotteries to be public nuisances; and all grants, patents, and licences, for such lotteries to be against law: they are also prohibited under penalties by Queen Ann.

It is not many years since the rage for insuring tickets during the drawing of a lottery, became so general, that hundreds of families, particularly of the lower orders of people, were annually ruined thereby: but in consequence of some late acts of Parliament for limiting the insurance of tickets, and regulating the lottery offices, under heavy penalties, which are rigorously enforced, this mischief is nearly rooted out.

By the existing statutes, all private lotteries by tickets, cards, or dice, and particularly the game of faro, basset, ace of hearts, hazard, passage, roly poly, and all other games with dice, except back-gammon, are prohibited under a penalty of £200. for him that shall erect such lotteries, unless by authority of Parliament. Lotteries were for many years drawn in Guildhall, but of late they have been removed to Cooper's Hall, in the City of London. It has always been customary for the scholars of Christ's Hospital, to draw the tickets out of the lottery wheels.

The annexed subject represents the manner of conveying the lottery wheels from Somerset Place, to Cooper's Hall. There are four sledges employed for this purpose, two carrying the wheels containing the tickets, and blanks and prizes, and the other two the cases for the wheels. They are escorted by a detachment of his Majesty's Life Guards.

Published by William Miller, Albemarle Street, Jan.y 1, 1805. No. 58.

PLATE LVIII.

BUTCHER.

IT appears to be generally admitted that no people cultivate the art of breeding, fattening, slaughtering, and preparing meat for the shambles, with so much care and success as the English; indeed the nature of English cookery demands this attention on the part of the butcher, &c. as nothing can be more plain and unsophisticated, or less likely to cover the defects of indifferent meat. There are many laws existing, which have been enacted in different reigns, for regulating this trade, the good effects of which are very generally evinced in the cleanliness and good state of our markets for butcher's meat.

Stowe, in speaking of Leadenhall-market, gives us an account of the habits and customs of the butchers of old times. "Forraine butchers," were not allowed to sell their meat in this market until the year 1533, when it was enacted that they should not sell their beef above a halfpenny the pound, and mutton a halfpenny half-farthing: "which act being devised for the commoditie of the realme, (as it was then thought) hath since proved far otherwayes;" for before that time a fat oxe was solde at London for sixe and twentie shillings eightpence, at the most; a fat weather for three shillings fourpence; a fat calfe the like price; a fat lambe for twelve pence; pieces of beefe weighed two pounds and a half at the least, yea three pound or better for a pennie, on every butcher's stall in this citie: and of those peeces of beef thirteen or fourteen for twelve pence; fat mutton for eightpence the quarter; and one hundred weight of beefe for four shillings eight pence, at the dearest: what the price is now I need not set down." There were, according to this historian, only sixe score butchers in the city and suburbs, of which every one killed six oxen each weekly, "which is in forty six weekes 33120, or 720 weekly." The foreign butchers, as they were called, stood in the high street of Limehouse ward, on the north side, twice a week, Wednesday and Saturday; but as the persons against whose houses they placed their blocks and stalls derived profit therefrom, they were admitted to occupy standings in Leadenhall, for which they paid to the chamber of the city.

The fraternity of butchers are of ancient standing, as they were fined for setting up an adulterine guild, without royal license in the reign of Henry the Second, anno 1180. They have a hall, and were incorporated by James the First, anno 1605. This company consists of a master, five wardens, twenty-one assistants, and two hundred and fourteen liverymen, who pay a fine of £2. each upon their admission into the livery.

Published by William Miller Albemarle Street, Jan.y 1.1805. No. 59.

PLATE LIX.

SHRIMPER.

SHRIMPS, of which abundance are daily eaten in London and places adjacent, are principally caught by women on the sands upon the sea-coast: these women are called Shrimpers, each of whom is provided with a net fixed to the end of a light pole. The manner of catching them is by the women tucking up their clothes, and going barefooted into the waves, where dipping the net in the shallow water, it is seldom raised without some of these diminutive inhabitants of the sea. The basket strapped to the waist is to receive them from the net. Great quantities are sent to the fish market at Billingsgate, in the neighbourhood of which coppers are kept, where they are boiled with salt, and are from thence disposed of to the fishmongers and others, who distribute them to the different parts of London, and circumjacent country.

The method of prawn-fishing differs from that of shrimping; the fisher is provided with three or four purse-nests fastened to iron-hoops, which are baited with crabs, stripped of the shell: these nets are dropped into holes upon rocky shores, and are floated with cork. The fisher carries a staff, forked at the end, which he uses to raise the nets after they have remained a sufficient time to have caught the prawns, who assemble therein to prey upon the crabs.

Published by William Miller, Albemarle Street, Jan.y 1.1805.

No. 60

PLATE LX.

HIGHLAND PIPER.

THE repeated changes which military dress has been subject to in every age amongst the English, and most other European troops, makes it remarkable that the Scottish military dress should so long have remained nearly the same. The short skirt scarcely covering the naked thighs, the cloak, chequered hose, and bonnet, being not very unlike what is represented to have been worn in the time of the Anglo-Romans, as appears by ancient sculptures that have been dug up in Great Britain at various places.

Another curious custom is preserved in each Scottish regiment, namely, that of having attached thereto players upon the bag-pipes, which instrument is supposed to be one of the most ancient now in use. This instrument consists of two principal parts; the first a leathern bag, which is filled with wind, by means of a little tube fitted to it, and stopped by a valve. The other part consists of three pipes or flutes, the first called the great pipe, or drone; the second, which passes the wind out at the bottom; and the third having a reed, is played on by compressing the bag under the arm when full, and by opening and stopping the holes, which are eight, with the fingers: the bagpipes take in the compass of three octaves. This instrument was called by the Romans utricularis tiba; and the players thereon, utriculari.

The highland regiments rank amongst the best troops in the service of the King of Great Britain: and the good discipline, steady conduct, patience, and bravery evinced by them in the campaigns of late, have rendered them deservedly dear to the English. Perhaps the present reign has been marked with no circumstance more grateful to humanity, than that of having united in the bonds of brotherly affection, the brave people of the two nations of England and Scotland.